THE NOVEL
A WRITER'S GUIDE

Discover the Joy
of Writing Fiction

Russell F. Moran

The Novel – A Writer's Guide – Discover the Joy of Writing Fiction

Coddington Press

DEDICATION

This book is dedicated to the *Indies*—the self-published authors of the world.

ACKNOWLEDGEMENTS

As always, I thank my wife, Lynda, for her attentive reading and rereading of my many drafts. For me, Lynda is one of the joys of writing fiction, even when she discovers my stupid mistakes. I also thank my friend and editor, John D. White, for his sharp-eyed proofreading, editing, and advice. And I especially thank my readers, many of whom are a constant source of inspiration and encouragement for me.

PREFACE

I wrote this book to inspire you, to encourage you, and maybe to nudge you to do something you've thought about for a long time—to write a novel. If you're like most people, you won't start the book; you will sit and *think* about writing the book; you will take long walks and think some more; you will bounce ideas off your spouse and friends; you will sit in a diner scribbling notes to yourself; you will do many of the things that novelists do, except for one thing—you won't start it. That's how books *don't* get written.

My primary audience is independent authors or self-publishers, also known as *Indies*. I'll go into more detail on the distinctions between self-publishing and traditional publishing later in Chapter Seven, but for now just know that a self-published author, or *Indie*, is a person who publishes her own book, while a traditionally published author is one who sells her manuscript to a publishing company.

I began my first novel, *The Gray Ship*, in 2012, and published it a year later in 2013. Since then I've written and published a total of 15 novels, with a 16th in draft 19 for final editing, a 17th in its 10th draft, and an 18th in first draft stage. I like to keep a bunch of pots cooking on the stove. You should too.

I've been writing all my life, having spent many years as a legal journalist and publisher, and I've also authored hundreds of articles on various subjects. I love to write, and I've been writing non-fiction for most of my life. I have one person to thank for encouraging me to write a novel, my wife, Lynda.

"When are you going to write that novel," Lynda asked, "when you get younger?"

That did it for me. No, I wasn't getting any younger. She made me realize that a novel could be, as it is for so many people, a dream that I'd get around to someday, or one that I should start working on—*now*.

And so, it began, on the back porch of our house on Long Island one warm June evening in 2012. What began was an adventure—and a magical experience.

Please allow me to share that enjoyment with you, and to be your cheerleader for bringing the thrill of writing fiction into your life. If you think you're missing something by not joining the ranks of storytellers, you're right.

Table of Contents

Chapter 1

What is the Magic of Writing Fiction?

I didn't know that writing fiction was enjoyable until I started doing it. Reread that sentence please and notice the words "doing it." Thinking or dreaming about writing a book won't cut it. You must *do it*. If you sit and stare at a blank canvas and think about painting, you're not an artist—you're a person *thinking* about becoming an artist.

When I decided to write my first novel, I had no idea of what was in store for me, intellectually or emotionally. After I came up with my outline (more about outlining later) and started to populate the story with characters, scenes, and chapters, something started to shift in my thinking. A novel, stripped down to its basics, is nothing more than a story, a story that's yours, one that you discovered in the dustbin of our collective unconsciousness.

I think of myself as a storyteller, and I recommend that you see yourself that way too. Human beings have been telling stories since we lived in caves. Recall the scene from the 1987 movie, *Quest for Fire*, where a group of cave dwellers regaled each other by "telling" a story about their recent mammoth hunt. Storytelling began with a few grunts and hand gestures and progressed to painting on cave walls. Eventually we became more sophisticated by carving on rocks, then wax tablets, then papyrus rolls, then paper, and now, in addition to paper, stories are told digitally on electronic devices in the form of ebooks, and aurally in the form of audible books. In the future, with the growth of Artificial Intelligence, maybe we'll tell stories by mental telepathy. I wouldn't try it today. Amazon is working on it, no doubt.

The shift in my thinking happened when I realized that my book was becoming a part of me, part of my everyday life. I felt as if my characters were walking around and talking to me. I was there—in the novel. As I slept I would dream about my characters, and I still do with each novel I write. Nightmares? Sure. If a scary character doesn't scare you, you haven't made him scary enough.

The characters, scenes, and chapters started to unfold in front of me. I can't emphasize that enough—the story *unfolds*. It isn't a simple process of telling your readers what happened scene after scene. It's a process where you're an active participant and also a witness to what's happening on the page. Yes, you're a witness. It's a magical experience, one that's hard to describe, but I'll try. *The Gray Ship*, my first novel, is a story of time travel and alternate history. Navy Captain Ashley Patterson, a 36-year-old African-American woman, is the commanding officer of the *USS California*, a nuclear-powered guided missile cruiser. A great deal of my research for the book consisted of meeting with my good friend, the late Admiral

Floyd (Hoss) Miller, the first commanding officer of the real *USS California*. Then the story began to unfold.

While steaming to Charleston, South Carolina, the *California* encounters a time portal, also known as a wormhole, and travels back in time from 2013 to 1861, two days before the beginning of the Civil War. Confederates who saw the *California* dubbed it *The Gray Ship*. In a scene where Captain Patterson meets Abraham Lincoln, I discovered that writing fiction is not just fun; it's magical. Abraham Lincoln, after his shock of meeting the lovely Captain Patterson, comes up with a history-changing idea of how the *California* can help the Union win the war, and win it fast, saving hundreds of thousands of lives. I won't spoil it for you in case you ever read *The Gray Ship*, but "his" idea was shattering. As I wrote the chapter I could swear that it was Abe Lincoln, not me, who came up with the plans. *That* was the magic—I was witnessing one of my characters, a historical figure, come up with fascinating ideas. While you're writing and rewriting your book you will notice that the story is constantly with you. You're not just making stuff up, you're living it, day by day. *Magic.*

Stephen King makes an analogy. He says that stories are like fossils—they already exist, and our job as storytellers is to uncover the fossil, sweep away the dirt, and expose what's there. I'm not sure if he was drawing an analogy or simply stating a timeless truth—that stories exist in our collective consciousness, or sub-consciousness, and the writer's job is to find them and bring them to life.

So, what is the magic? It comes in a lot of different ways. I discussed my life-shifting experience with my first novel, and it continued with every novel I've written since.

Recently I received an email from a stranger I had met a few weeks before. I attended a book signing event at a country fair along with my friends and colleagues from the Long Island Author's Group. I sold only nine books that day, but one sale I'll never forget. In the morning, a woman bought my first book, *The Gray Ship*. I explained to her that it was the first of seven books in the *Time Magnet Series*. About two hours passed by and the woman came up to the table again. "I love it," she said. "I've only read four chapters, but I want to buy the next one while you're still here." She actually couldn't wait to read the book, so she sat down on a bench and started to dig into the story. She then bought the sequel to *The Gray Ship*, *The Thanksgiving Gang*. My new friend made my day. Not only did she start to read the first book, but came back to the table and bought the next one.

To be told that somebody loved my book—while reading it—was a thrill, but it gets even better. A few days later, I got an email from the woman asking me to send her the next two books in the series. She wanted to buy them directly from me rather than through Amazon, because she wanted my autographed copies. Again—magic—it's that simple. A perfect stranger had become a fan. My words had touched somebody and made a difference.

Chapter 2

How do you start? Where do you start?

Stephen King, in his semi-autobiographical book *On Writing: A Memoir of The Craft,* says there are four types of writers: bad writers, competent writers, good writers, and great writers. King humbly refers to himself as a good writer, but sorry, some of his work is great, pure genius.

According to Master Stephen, "While it is *impossible* to make a competent writer out of a bad writer, and while it is equally impossible to make a great writer out of a good one, *it is possible, with lots of hard work, dedication, and timely help, to make a good writer out of a merely competent one.*" (Emphasis added). King, Stephen (2000-10-03). *On Writing: A Memoir of The Craft* (Kindle Locations 1714-1716). Scribner. Kindle Edition.

I found those words motivating, and I still do. I know I'm a competent writer, having successfully published articles and nonfiction books for many years. I strive to be good, and I think I get there, at least occasionally. But I do not try to be great, and neither should you, because you and I have no control over it. Greatness is either in you or it's not, and it takes a hell of a lot more than practice. It's a genetic thing. No matter how many baskets I shoot, I'm not going to be Michael Jordan.

No matter how many times I whack at the marble, it's unlikely that Michelangelo's *David* will appear.

So that's where I started, and probably where you're starting as well. I knew that I was competent, and my goal was to become good. If you're a bad writer, you probably aren't reading this book. But, that said, there are a lot of bad writers out there inflicting literary graffiti upon the reading world. The better news is that if you're a competent writer, becoming a good writer is within your reach. But note that King emphasizes that the transition requires *"lots of hard work, dedication, and timely help."* It isn't easy, but it's doable, and it's a joy. I had a lot of help, and the book you're reading is one part of the sequence—help.

Chapter 3

The Road to a Novel

All novels go through the same basic process. *All* novels, not just some.

1. **The idea**. An idea can result from a visual prompt, a scene, a broken-down truck, a quarrel in a restaurant. Somebody insulted you or praised you. Quick, think about that incident and recall your feelings when it happened. Maybe you have some ideas about your high school days. My book, *A Reunion in Time,* showed up in my mind as I drove past my old high school. What would it be like to go back there by traveling through time? Ideas flow from our human experience. Sometimes an idea for a novel may be a random observation, such as my old high school, or it can be the result of a wandering mind, or a brainstorming session with a friend or spouse. Stephen King writes about slipping on a hill outside a gas station in rural Pennsylvania. Had he continued to slip, he would have fallen into a fast-moving creek. He wondered how long it would have taken the gas station attendant to realize he was missing. That simple event resulted in his book, *From a Buick 8.* The idea for *The*

Gray Ship, my first novel, came out of a conversation with my wife, Lynda. The idea was a modern warship that travels through time to the Civil War.

2. **The Concept**. An idea is just the spark. From that spark it's necessary to develop the idea into a concept for a book, a more fully developed set of ideas. *I was swept away in a creek and nobody knew I was missing*—that's a concept. Or, in the case of *The Gray Ship*, an African-American woman commands a modern warship in the Civil War. I still recall the excitement I felt when I came up with that concept—on my back porch, having a cocktail with Lynda. I served in the Navy aboard a warship, and parts of the concept flowed from my own experience (although not in the Civil War). Writing the book required my brain to travel through time.

3. **The Story**. A concept, when fully developed, results in the objective of any novelist—a story. That's what a novel is, a story. It has a beginning, a crisis of some sort to give the hero something to fight for or against, a plot which shows how it all fits together, and finally the end, where the hero slays the dragons. The dragons can be, well, dragons, or they can be emotional dragons, like drugs or alcohol, divorce, depression, or cancer. I recently slew that last one, with the help of some talented doctors. I may write a novel about the experience some day. Maybe, but there isn't a hell of a lot of magic in writing about chemotherapy.

4. The Plot. The word plot means the events that make up a story. The events must relate to each other in a pattern or a logical sequence. The structure of your novel depends on how you organize the events in the plot of the story. Some novels contain plots that go back and forth between the present and the past—or maybe the future. Others are organized with alternating chapters that are narrated by two major protagonists. Don't get hung up on the plot. It's really just the way that you organize the events to make a compelling story.

How I began the journey to my first novel

As I mentioned in the preface, *The Gray Ship* began on the back porch of my house during a conversation with my wife, Lynda. You will often hear the suggestion, especially by new authors, that you should write about things you know. So, Lynda asked me what I knew about. We came up with a list: the law (I'm a lawyer and spent many years as a legal journalist. I had also written a nonfiction book on the law, *Justice in America: How it Works-How it Fails*); I'm a Navy veteran and have always been interested in things military and nautical; I'm a Civil War buff; I ran a legal periodical publishing business for many years. So, I had some basic background to work with. I homed in first on the law, which seemed like a natural. But I decided that I wanted something a bit more adventurous. Since then I've published *Sideswiped* and *The Reformers*, and *The President is Missing*, my first legal thrillers. Please don't confuse *The President is Missing* with a book of the same title by James Patterson and

William Clinton. Mine was published over a year before theirs. No, you can't copywrite a book title.

I remembered the book and the movie *The Final Countdown*, which starred Kirk Douglas as a captain of a nuclear aircraft carrier that slipped through a time portal and found itself at the beginning of World War II. So, how about a nuclear guided-missile cruiser commanded by an African-American woman that hits a time portal and winds up near Fort Sumter just before the Civil War began? That was the **concept**. Within a week after coming up with the idea, I came upon Captain Ashley Patterson, or as Stephen King might say, I discovered her while working on the concept. I didn't know where the concept was headed at the time, but that was okay. I had an idea and a concept that would lead to the **story**.

So how does a story unfold in a way that people want to read it? How does a simple idea and a concept result in a book with characters, scenes, a plot, sub-plots, and a conclusion? This question brings us to the great debate among literary pundits.

Outliners, Pansters, and In-Betweeners

An excellent writer on the subject of the structure of a novel is Larry Brooks, the author of *Story Engineering*. In the book he dissects what a novel is all about, addresses the core competencies that a writer needs, and the basic structure of a novel. I consider it a must-read for any fiction writer. Brooks discerns that there are two types of writers, an outliner and a "panster," meaning one who writes by the seat of his pants. I add a third, the "in-betweener" (that's me, and most writers I know).

Outliners - Some writers insist that the only way to begin a novel is to first write a detailed outline, and Brooks comes down heavily on this side. Once you've written your detailed outline, you then consult the outline, and write your characters and the scenes according to the framework that you've already established. The logic behind this idea is compelling. How can you write a novel unless you first see the framework of the story? It's also easier to write the book, outliners insist, because you have a framework to consult when beginning to hammer out your first draft. A friend of mine is a strong advocate of this way of writing. She's the author of books for the YA or young adult market. A former teacher, she comes from a strong scientific background. For her, outlining is in her blood, and her scenes flow in a logical way. She is the only novelist I personally know who is a strict outliner. James Patterson, one of the best-selling authors of all time, is also a proponent of outlining. He says that he will revise and rewrite an outline dozens of times before he begins to write the story. In the early stages of one of his novels, he hasn't begun the book yet, but keeps reviewing and revising the outline.

Pansters - Those who write from the seat of their pants can't be bothered with outlines, primarily because they believe it stunts the creative process. A panster relies on the "muse" to provide characters, scenes, and details as he writes. Let the thoughts and words flow, pansters insist, and it will all come out in the end. But, as the English novelist Robert Graves said,

"There is no such thing as good writing, only good rewriting." If your book will go through multiple rewrites, the panster insists, why trouble yourself with an outline because you'll be rewriting anyway. But, as Brooks points out in *Story Engineering*, such a process can be agonizingly laborious. It's almost as if you are simultaneously working on multiple books at the same time. Writing can be replaced by drudgery, especially if the writer decides to completely revise the story after he's written the first draft. A good outline makes for a good story and it makes the process flow smoothly. If you are constantly rewriting your entire novel, your head will begin to spin, and you will feel lost. You'll experience frustration, and there's no joy in that, no magic.

In-Betweeners - I wish I could be an outliner, I really do. I *am* an outliner when writing nonfiction, such as this book, but for writing fiction I've come to a conclusion: I outline as I go. The reason I don't outline an entire story from scratch is because I'm simply unable to do that. I *don't know the entire story yet*. I have a strong concept in mind and a general idea of where the story will go, but only by starting to write do I understand the book and watch the story unfold. For me, and this may be so for you as well, the *story unfolds as I write it*. Most writers I talk to feel the same way. I don't know the whole story in advance and that's why I'm not a traditional outliner. In any of the novels I've written I never knew the ending when I started the book, other than a general idea of how the story would turn out. In one of my books I killed the major protagonist, something I never thought I'd do at the beginning of the novel.

I've tried outlining and gave up in frustration, because the characters in the story would suddenly take me in a different direction and screw up my outline. For me, the thrill comes from the creative process, from seeing how characters act, the scenes they get involved in, and how they confront and solve problems. But I am not a panster. I don't just sit down at my keyboard and let the muse take over. I outline *as I write*, keeping a chapter outline open on a separate computer screen. Sometimes, when the story points the way, I will write a few chapter headings in advance of where I am, but usually the next chapter is dictated by the story as developed so far. Stephen King writes much the same way. He says that you should populate the first draft with characters and then follow those characters as they take you in different directions. To me, that's the magic.

How do I begin? Days in advance of actually sitting down to write the story, I make detailed notes on a yellow pad. Often, I'll have 10 or 20 pages of notes before I begin to write. This is not as structured as an outline, but it works, in a somewhat sloppy way. Some call these notes "beats," as in music. I constantly write down beats or ideas every day for a novel I'm planning. VERY IMPORTANT—When an idea hits you, write it down. Few things in life are more frustrating than to sit down to write, and that wonderful idea that popped into your head earlier isn't there anymore. As you jot down your ideas, and in the early stages of writing your book, I recommend doing this alone and not sharing it with anybody, including your spouse or partner. Lynda, for example, is one of my primary editors. I want to spring the whole story on her at once, and she prefers that too.

What if? The Writer's Improv

I always begin with the greatest question a writer can ask: "What if?" What if she saw her girlfriend's phone number in her husband's wallet? What if the man with the answers was killed? What if the gun wasn't loaded? What if it was? What if the captain of the ship changes history? What if he didn't love her as she thought, but intended to kill her? What if the boss, or general, or admiral, develops sudden-onset Alzheimer's? Writers have a lot to learn from improvisational comedy, or "improv." The basic rule of improv is that the actor whose turn it is never disagrees with or blocks the suggestion made by his improv partner. The answer is always "yes," although seldom spoken. Just assume a "yes" and go on. Don't fight it, don't intellectualize it, just go for it. An improv actor might say to his partner, "I think I'm going to shoot you." Bad improv would be for the other guy to resist, to say no. But a good actor would say something like, "Well, I can't say I blame you, but let's have a beer first." It's similar to brainstorming, the basic rule of which is never to ignore an idea. Critique comes later. Just write it down, even if it seems stupid at first. Asking the question "what if" *draws ideas out of your brain.* Almost all the notes or beats on my yellow pad are responses to the question, "what if?" Note that I say they're responses, not answers. The most typical response to a "what if" question is another what if. Here are some of my initial "what if" questions that I jotted down before I began *The Gray Ship:*

- What if the ship goes through a time portal and ends up at the beginning of the Civil War?
- What if the ship was commanded by beautiful young African-American woman?
- What if a crew member knows the secrets to the time portal or wormhole?
- What if he's a young, handsome widower?
- What if the captain, a widow, falls in love with the sailor?
- What if the captain meets Abraham Lincoln?
- What if the captain is instrumental in ending slavery?

This is the joy of writing fiction, the magic. Had I not come up with those questions I would have laboriously dreamed up a story line. Again, the idea behind *The Gray Ship* was a warship traveling through time. The concept was a ship that traveled to the Civil War, commanded by beautiful young African-American woman. Then came *The Story*, which emerged from "what if" questions. Sure, I came up with the characters, but before I began to write, they weren't people, just names and their role in the story. Don't worry, you won't have to wrack your brain to create characters—they'll show up when needed. Who are these people? People you like, people you don't, people you've dreamed about, people you've seen in movies or read about in books, or seen on TV in handcuffs being led to jail. You will often hear a novelist say that a scene writes itself. This is true, and is part of the magic of writing fiction. In one of the pivotal scenes in *The Gray Ship,* Abraham Lincoln came up with an idea that became an irreplaceable part of the story.

That's right, Abe Lincoln thought of it. As I mentioned before, I just wrote what his character dictated. I know that sounds crazy, but it's true. I found myself thinking of Lincoln and saying to myself, "hey, that's a great idea." Lincoln came up with the idea because the story propelled him toward it. What I just said is different from a writer who looks to an outline and says, now this happens, then that happens, and then this happens. No, let the story take you there. Let it *unfold*. That's the magic of writing fiction.

Chapter 4

Covers and Titles

I'm discussing covers and titles early in this book, because they're important. Often, however, you won't decide on a title until you're well into writing your story. The title of *The Gray Ship*, when I began the book, was *Fort Sumpter, 2013*. I think *The Gray Ship* is much better. That title showed up somewhere in my fifth draft as I recall.

In this chapter, I assume that you are going to self-publish your book. If you go the traditional route of finding a publishing company to bring your book to the public, you can make suggestions, but the cover and title decision will be made by someone else.

Covers

"You can't tell a book from its cover." So, goes the old cliché. But writers know that the cliché is wrong. Yes, you *can* tell a book by its cover, and that's what readers do. The cover of your novel is one of those critical points on your road to publication. Chances are strong that you're not the one to design it. Unless you're a trained graphic artist, don't try to design your own cover. Ignore what I just said if you believe you have the talent. Give it a try and show your work to others for opinions. The whole purpose behind a good cover is to get a potential reader (and buyer) to pick up your book or to click the image online. The cover won't describe the story, of course, but it gives the reader an inkling of what he can expect. Cover design prices range from less than a hundred dollars to thousands for an A-list designer. When you use a cover designer, you must first communicate your thoughts on the content of your book. I always write the *back-cover description* before contacting a designer, and I submit that description along with my thoughts.

The words on the back of your book are important, whether it's a brief description of the story, or even better, some snippets from positive reviews. Think of the back cover as your selling space. I've seen some inexperienced self-published authors leave the back empty except for artwork. That is pure insanity. It's your chance to get a person to open the book. Why would somebody open the book if he doesn't have any idea of what the story is about? That's the purpose of the words on the back cover—to briefly describe the story, or a bunch of paragraphs showing why other people loved it.

How much is a good cover designer worth? This is an entirely subjective question. I have seen covers on self-published books that, in my opinion, are far superior to covers you see on *The New York Times* bestseller list from major publishing houses. There are countless books and online courses devoted to book covers. Reading about this subject can be as annoying as listening to a wine connoisseur prattle on about a new vintage. "This Bordeaux has curious presumptions and subtle humorous undercurrents." What?

My criteria for a good cover is that it shows an **element of mystery**, a design that will pique a browser's curiosity.

Can you save money and still get a well-done cover? Yes, and I suggest that you consider *premade book covers*. Take a look at www.thebookcoverdesigner.com, a somewhat clumsily named website but one that tells you exactly what you can expect. The company uses a small army of professional cover designers who get paid a percentage if you buy one of the templates. These premade designs include artwork and made-up words, including an author's name and title, that show you the font, font size, and contrast with the background color. You must supply the title, subtitle if any, how you want your name to appear, and the words for the back cover. Once you've bought it, the cover is retired and nobody else can use it. The prices range from $30 to a couple of hundred dollars. Make sure that the person you're buying the template from includes the design for a paperback spine and back cover, *not just the front cover* for an ebook. Some of the artists charge a few dollars extra to include a paperback-ready design, and it's worth it because the design needs to be tweaked to fit your chosen paperback trim size and number of pages. The beauty of using a service like this is that you can look for a cover that captures the essence of your novel, one that *jumps out at you*. I've used a professional designer for eleven novels and two non-fiction books at a cost of $250 for each cover. For one of my recent books, *Robot Depot*, I used a premade template that cost $40.

A word about trim size. The industry standard for a trade paperback is six by nine inches (6'x9'). Unless you have a strong reason, such as a children's book, I suggest that you stick with the standard trim size. I recently purchased a stand-up display rack to show my books at speaking engagements and book signing events. Each space on the rack designed to accommodate the standard 6/9 trim size. If you vary too much from the standard, be prepared to design your own display stands.

I always circulate a few designs among friends and ask their opinion. I would rather get the opinions of potential readers not cover designers. This is "fair use," so don't worry about copyright infringement.

Titles

The title of a novel is not as important as the title of a nonfiction book. In nonfiction you need to give a strong idea about the content of the book, such as *Astrophysics for People in a Hurry*. The subject of that best seller is, you guessed it, astrophysics. By including the somewhat humorous words, "for People in a Hurry" the author tells you that the book is written for the layperson, not necessarily a physicist. The title of a novel, on the other hand, doesn't need to describe what's inside, but I think it's good style to *hint* at the contents. If nothing else, it will enable the reader to recall the name of your book when recommending it to somebody. In one of my novels, *The Thanksgiving Gang,* the title doesn't make sense until you're a few chapters into the book, but then it makes a lot of sense—a bunch of people who are trying to prevent a horrible disaster on Thanksgiving Day. Don't feel bad if you have a hard time coming up with a title. It's not unusual for me to change the title *after* I've finished writing the book.

Chapter 5

---✦---

What Format? Ebook, Paperback, Hardcover, Audiobook

This chapter assumes your book will be self-published. If not, the format decision won't be yours.

Whether to self-publish or go the traditional route of trying to find a publisher is covered in detail in Chapter Seven.

I put the word hardcover in the title of this chapter, but I strongly advise you as a self-publisher to forget about a hardcover book, unless you regularly turn out best sellers. It's just too expensive. The big players in the self-publishing business, like Createspace (which is now part of Kindle Direct Publishing) don't even offer hardcover as a choice, although Ingram Spark does.

Publishing your novel as an ebook is a no-brainer. It's quite easy to format and upload to Kindle. I say it's a no-brainer to publish your work as an electronic book or ebook because the cost is low to nothing. A large portion of the reading public prefers ebooks, so this is a gotta-do-it. A reader doesn't even have to buy a Kindle device. All he needs do is download the FREE Kindle software to a PC, a cell phone, or an IPad. Amazon won't let anything get in its way as it conquers the world. Barnes and Noble competes with Amazon Kindles with its Nook.

The real choice many self-published authors struggle with is whether to publish it as a paperback at all, or just leave it as an ebook. There are two problems with publishing only as an ebook. The first concern is that you're obviously eliminating paper readers if all you've got is a digital book. In my experience, the majority of people I talk to prefer the look and feel of a paper book. Studies bear out my subjective experience. As you will see in Chapter Seven about the publishing revolution, the initial popularity of ebooks has leveled and is now falling. The second problem with publishing only as an ebook is that you can't attend book-signing events, excellent occasions for getting your name and your book out there. With paperbacks, you can carry a supply in your car. I once met a friend at a diner, and the conversation got around to my books. I often gently nudge conversations that way (while struggling valiantly not to be obnoxious). My friend said, "I'd love to buy that one." Instant gratification. I just went to my car and personally delivered an autographed copy to her.

Another problem with the ebook-only route is that your novel will never appear in a library or bookstore. If you're asked to give a talk at a local library or Rotary Club, without a paper book to wave around you'll be just a talking head.

So, to me, there is no real choice. You should publish an ebook, which is easy and cheap, and you should *also publish a paperback.* A fact of life is that you and I can't control the market. Therefore, we need to give the market what it wants.

THE NOVEL A WRITER'S GUIDE

And it wants both ebooks and hard-copy books. The market also demands audiobooks as we'll see in the next section

Audiobooks

Of the major changes in the publishing industry, there is one area that's experiencing enormous growth. From 2016 to 2017 *ebook sales have gone down a whopping 12 percent*, but sales of audiobooks are exploding. According to the authoritative *Good e-Reader Audiobook Report*, the past few years have shown that audiobooks are the fastest growing segment of the publishing industry. The global audiobook industry is currently valued at 3.5 billion dollars, and the United States is currently the largest part of the market with 1.8 billion dollars in audio sales in 2016. That's an incredible *31% increase from 2015.*

See the report at https://goodereader.com/blog/digital-publishing/audiobook-trends-and-statistics-for-2017.

Just look at the raw numbers of audiobooks produced over the past few years:

- 2007 – 3,037 audiobooks created
- 2012 – 16, 309 audiobooks created
- 2016 – 50,937 audiobooks created

As I'm writing this, I realize that audiobook publishing is an area that I've been ignoring, but no more. My research on the audiobook market tells me that I must go there, and so should you. Later in this book toward the end of Chapter Nine, I discuss the competition we face, not from other writers, but from the endless choices for our leisure time. Television is no longer a "vast wasteland," but a source of quality entertainment, and our TV viewing is encouraged by round-the-clock news programs on cable TV. Our cell phones and iPads scream at us to pay attention to the latest text, email, ballgame score, or breaking news report.

Audiobooks, typically listened to over your cell phone, give us Americans the thing we seem to love—the ability to multitask. Whether it's driving our cars, walking, jogging, doing the laundry, or emptying the dishwasher, we can "read" our favorite books with our ears. I've listened to Stephen King, J.K. Rowling, and other great authors while walking the deck on a cruise ship. The A-list authors have their books narrated by A-list narrators, but some authors opt to narrate their own books, with mixed results.

Times are changing for us Indies as well. You can produce an audiobook with a reasonable outlay of money using a variety of services. A narrator's fee can vary from under $100 per hour to several hundred. **A rule of thumb** for you to work with—Figure that the production time for "a finished hour" is about 9,000 words per hour. So, a book with 100,000 words should equal 11 hours. If the narrator charges $350 per finished hour, which some commentators say is the standard rate, you will pay $3,850, about the price of a non-A-list editor.

Some narrators are willing to work on spec, meaning they will get a percentage of sales, and you are tied to them for seven years. A typical "on spec" deal will require you to pay a small up-front fee, and then a percentage of sales for the narrator and the company you're dealing with, assuming you go through one of the big outfits like ACX. That company, an Amazon subsidiary of course, gives you the choice of paying up front or paying the narrator a percentage of the royalty, usually 50 percent. While you don't need to lay out money up front, you may wind up paying more for the percentage of sales approach over the long run. Of course, the seller, such as Amazon, gets a cut too. See Findvoices.com for an excellent Q&A. That company, however, will not use spec deals, opting instead to pay its narrators hourly as discussed above.

Do It Yourself Audiobooks

Another way to create an audiobook is to narrate it yourself. But beware—you should be honest with yourself and ask if you have the talent to do so. If you have a good voice and a flair for acting, go for it. But don't think you can dictate into a little hand-held recording device. Just like any segment of our technology driven world, the audiobook industry has a lot of moveable parts, and some of those parts are complicated.

What you need is some good (not necessarily expensive) equipment and audio editing software. I recently purchased an excellent microphone—Audio-Technica ATR2100, for $64; a good pair of earphones—Sennheiser HD 202 II for $57, and a "pop filter" from Neewer for $6.99. The pop filter is essential. It's a doohickey that goes in front of your microphone and cuts out the "p" and "b" sounds that your lips make.

Your real challenge is mastering the editing software, known as a DAW, for Digital Audio Workstation. One of the biggest players is Audacity, which is a free open source program. It costs nothing, and like most free programs it comes with a piss-poor help desk. Have a question? Go to the forum and try to figure out what other people have discovered about your issue. Voice **editing** is essential, unless you want to inflict your hiccups and deep breaths on your listeners.

Next to Audacity is Pro Tools from Avid, which many commentators say is the industry standard. They provide a free version, which I tried to install but gave up after seven attempts. When I called them, the support person told me that I would have to purchase a paid version for $299, payable monthly in $24.95 increments. You cannot cancel if you don't like it, and are on the hook for $299, even if you're unable to install it. A new frontier in customer service.

A complete review of self-narrating is beyond the scope of this book, and frankly, beyond my expertise as I'm just learning. As you would expect, there are a ton of video courses on how to narrate your own book, as well as how to use the various DAWs. Just go to Youtube and put in the search string "how to narrate your own book," or "how to edit an audiobook with a DAW." I suggest that you stick to videos less than a year old to make sure you're working with the most recent version of the software as the people in the videos. Once you have narrated your book, you can find audio editors if you want to skip the editing part. It's a bit complicated to edit your voice with any of the DAWs, but it's necessary to at least do the initial editing of your mistakes. You may also want to find a person to convert your audacity files to MP3 format so you can upload to ACX when you're ready to go into production. I suggest

ACX as the natural choice. Go to ACX.com and look at their requirements.

If you have a good voice for narration but don't want the technical headaches of editing your own voice, you can outsource the job to an audiobook editor. Check out the many audio editors on fiverr.com. You will spend a lot more than five dollars.

Think of narrating your book as one round of proofreading. Because it's a good practice to read your manuscript aloud when editing, using the time to narrate your own book is like *killing two birds with one stone.* Did I mention that you should avoid worn-out clichés?

Of the 20 books I've published, five of them are nonfiction. I intend to self-narrate all my nonfiction books. For my novels, I'm not sure that I will narrate them, because I don't know if I have the acting talent to speak in a woman's voice, and then switch to a male. In *The Gray Ship,* for example, Captain Ashley Patterson, a woman, has a crisp military voice, except if she's talking to the guy she's in love with, when her voice softens as she asks for a kiss. The other characters in the book speak in a variety of voices, including Abraham Lincoln. So, for nonfiction, it's a no-brainer for me to self-narrate. I'm still on a journey of discovery for self-narrating my novels. I'm going to circulate samples to friends and listen to their advice.

A good narrator, and maybe that's you (or me), can switch from a male to a female-sounding voice by changing the pitch and octave. A male, for example, shouldn't use a falsetto voice to try to sound exactly like a woman or it can make for unintentional humor. Think Dustin Hoffman in *Tootsie* or Jack Lemmon in *Some Like It Hot*. Once you've listened to a couple of chapters, the changing voices become natural. I listened to Stephen King's *Mr. Mercedes*, read by Will Patton, a narrator with Audible.com. Patton won the *Best Male Narrator Audie Award*. Besides the voices of men, he also spoke as a young boy and a variety of women. Let's face it, you can't hire a platoon of voice actors for all your characters. If you've decided to look for a narrator other than yourself, you get to audition the narrators, first by listening to a sample on their website, and then listen to them reading a page or two from your book.

The most popular audiobook genres in 2016 were mystery, thriller, romance, and fantasy/science fiction, similar the popular genres of ebooks.

Audible is the biggest audiobook retailer with over 325,000 audio titles available.

You can shop around, but it's probably a good idea to go with the industry leader. ACX (for Audiobook Creation Exchange), a division of Audible.com, which is owned by, surprise, surprise, Amazon. Another fine company, one that caters to Indie authors, is Findawayvoices.com, mentioned above. Cute name, but a serious player, except they don't have narrators who will work on spec. The field is changing fast, as you would expect in an industry segment that is booming. You can find discussions by the big names in the field in the report I discussed above.

See the report here:

https://goodereader.com/blog/digital-publishing/audiobook-trends-and-statistics-for-2017.

So, listen, pardon my pun. All your novels should be in ebook and print formats, as well as the fast-growing audiobook format. You've already done the hard part—writing your book. Add on a few complications and narrate it yourself or pay a professional narrator to do it for you. Publishing your work as an audiobook only makes sense.

Chapter 6

The Style Sheet – Don't Write Without It

A style sheet for writing a novel can mean different things. For a publishing house, the sheet will include font, typeface, font size, colors, and various other essential details for a book to launch. But for the purpose here, I mean a much simpler document, simple but important. Think of a style sheet as a guide to your book. A style sheet is necessary whether or not you have a paid editor (and you should have an editor as I discuss later). But even if you don't hire an editor, a style sheet is a valuable aid to help you write your book. It will save you enormous amounts of time, and each draft will be much better for it. Once it's done, you can use a lot of your style sheet for your future books, especially the part of the sheet that concerns grammatical conventions, which don't usually change from book to book. You don't write an entire style sheet before starting your book, but as you go. For certain elements that will appear in any book you write, such as grammatical and spelling conventions, just copy from your standard style sheet and paste those parts into the style sheet for book you're working on. A style sheet is more than just style, and here's what it should include:

Characters, with details on their age, appearance, and mannerisms, in other words, the things you say about them in your book, and even some attributes that don't wind up in the book. It's the first step to creating a real person for your readers, as well as yourself. It's a way for you to really get to know the character, so the next time she shows up in a scene, you don't have to reimagine what she looks or acts like. "Bob looked into Jane's beautiful blue eyes." (or were they brown?)—Just glance at Jane in your style sheet. As you get deeper into your novel, you will forget a lot of things. Believe me, it happens. Suddenly, on page 85, Ben may appear in your mind as fat, but on page 10 you talk about how skinny he is. Either put him on a diet or eliminate the word "fat" on page 85. Style sheet to the rescue. All you need to do is look at the character description on your style sheet. This beats the hell out of doing a search back through the book, especially if it's a character who appears often. The character part of the style sheet will include stuff that doesn't show up in the book, things your reader will never see, but things that are imprinted on your brain. The purpose is to flesh out the character in your mind so that you can insert him easily into a scene. Buster, a character who appears in many of my books, is easy to fit into a scene. It's easy because I have a complete description in my style sheet, so I know what he's likely to do in any scenario. It also helps make your novel more believable and consistent, both of which are essential. In my books I include a list of characters, but it consists only of name and identification, not the detailed character description that I put in my style sheet. Here are a few character descriptions for my style sheet for *The Scent of Revenge,* which was published in the summer of 2015.

Characters - The Scent of Revenge

Auletta, Barbara—55 years old 5'11" tall, short brown hair, blue eyes. She's pretty and polite, but is a hard-nosed FBI division head. She came up through the ranks. A tough task master but easy to get along with. She cares about the welfare of the agents who work for her, but isn't afraid to pull the trigger on a bad guy.

Bellamy, Ellen—Rick's wife. She's 38 years old, a prominent architect, has medium length blond hair, and pale green eyes. Ellen's a fitness nut, and has the figure to show for it. Under her left eye is a slight scar from a fall she took as a kid, and it shows up as a dimple when she smiles. She has a warmth about her that just kind of radiates. She cares about people, even strangers. Close to husband Rick. Frisky love life.

Bellamy, Rick—42-year-old FBI agent in charge of counterterrorism. Works at 26 Federal Plaza in NYC. Former Marine captain. 6'2". Dedicated, takes job seriously, and pops a lot of Maalox. Obsessed with connecting dots and tracking patterns. Deeply in love with his wife, Ellen.

Buchannan, Frank—Epidemiologist who tracks dementia cases. Buchannan, age 45, is a slim, studious intellectual looking guy, about 6'3" with reading glasses permanently ensconced on the end of his nose. He has close cropped brown hair. Shocks people when he uncharacteristically drops f-bombs.

Burns, Olga—Private duty nurse who tends to people with dementia. Olga's a tall, heavy-set woman with a ready smile. About 45 years old. She speaks with a Ukrainian accent. Likeable, loyal, and trustworthy. She calls Rick, "Meester Reek."

Buster—aka Agent Charles Atkins, aka Gamal Akhbar, aka a lot of other aliases. 45 years old. 6 feet tall, well-built with swarthy Middle Eastern complexion. Short black hair. Says he has no time to comb his hair so he keeps it short. He's a Coptic Christian and a top spy with the CIA. People call him a human action figure: He gets things done—fast. He thinks and acts 10 moves ahead. Fluent in Arabic—his parents are Egyptian. Good friend of Rick Bellamy and Bennie Weinberg. Brilliant at tracking down clues.

McMartin, Trevor—Trevor's a bank examiner from Australia. He's been hired by Angus MacPherson. Angus called and suggested they get together. Bellamy worked with Trevor before, and is been amazed at his money tracking skills. Math and computer genius and gets paid a fortune. Wears Savile Row suits. Greets people with "G'day, Mates." Also refers to men as "blokes."

Pushkin, Dmitri—He's a chemical engineer and a professor at Chechen State University in Grozny, Chechnya—known as 'the chemist." A radical Islamist, he was involved in a lot of attacks on Russians. Ruthless—doesn't care who he kills.

Reynolds, William—President of the United States. Reynolds is a big man, about 6'3", with broad shoulders. He cuts a commanding figure. He likes Rick Bellamy and the feeling is mutual. Good sense of humor. Tough and smart. Cusses a lot.

Watson, Sarah—FBI director. Good leader. Has a reputation for insisting that meetings start on time. Watson can get testy as hell when anybody's late for a meeting, but she is also friendly and takes care of her people. Good sense of humor. Cusses occasionally.

Weinberg, Bennie—Dr. Benjamin Weinberg, a psychiatrist and detective with the NYPD, was on loan to the FBI. Bennie is nationally famous for his skills in detecting lies, especially from people on the witness stand. Bennie is short at 5'8," slightly overweight, and has a bald spot on the top of his head, but he does NOT cover it with a comb over. After he graduated from Harvard Medical School, Bennie served as a combat physician in the Army during the first Gulf War. Along with his academic credentials, Ben is an expert marksman. He's popular with prosecutors across the country. His nickname, which he hates, is Bennie-the-Bullshit-Detector. Although his academic credentials would lead you to think he'd come across as an intellectual, Bennie opts for the tough demeanor of a cop. His sentences are copiously sprinkled with f-bombs. He's also a good friend of Rick and Buster. A tough SOB when he needs to be.

Imagine an editor, or yourself for that matter, not having these character descriptions on a style sheet.

Facts, Grammatical Notes, and Conventions—*The Scent of Revenge* Style Sheet

Here you list things and places that show up often, as well as the grammatical conventions that you follow. I use the *Chicago Manual of Style*, but sometimes I adopt one of its allowable exceptions. The key here is *consistency,* one of the major benefits of a style sheet. I spell counterterrorism as one word, although you sometimes see it as two. The entries below are from the style sheet for *The Scent of Revenge.*

Facts, and Grammatical Notes, and Conventions

- 128 Walton Street, Baltimore—*Scent of Revenge* factory
- al-Qaeda (although *The New York Times* style sheet changes it every two days)
- Age—a 10-year-old (hyphens). 10 years old, no hyphens.
- Apostrophes after plural words—No double "s." e.g. – "The Reynolds' car is new," not "The Reynolds's car…"
- Articles in magazines or newspapers are in quotes not italics. The name of the publication itself is in italics.
- Book titles – Italicize
- Cellphone – one word
- Commas—Use serial or Oxford comma. "I bought bread, cheese, and wine."
- Counterterrorism – one word
- Jihadi, jihadis—A terrorist who wages a holy struggle or jihad. Not capitalized.

- Numbers—Use commas for four or more digits – 1,600 not 1600 (unless it's an address such as 1600 Pennsylvania Avenue). Spell out numbers one through nine, and also numbers that begin a sentence.
- Official titles—Lowercase unless it's in the person's title—
- Preventive, not preventative
- Publications—Italicize as in *The New York Times.*
- Ship names—Italicize—*Ocean Ecstasy, USS Gideon Welles, S.S. Cape Orlando*
- Slang words ending in "g"—Drop the "g" and *no apostrophe*—friggin, botherin
- The Committee—Organization of ISIS and al-Qaeda big shots
- Time—a.m. or p.m. Some like capital letters. Be consistent.
- TV Shows—Italicize, as in *The Ellen Bellamy Show* or *Barney the Dinosaur*

The Timeline

Nothing is easier to screw up than the timing of events as they occur in your novel. If you have a character chatting two weeks after he was killed, you've messed up. It's simple and important. Just do it. The following is the timeline from *The Scent of Revenge.*

Timeline – The Scent of Revenge

- March 1, 2016—Ellen comes up with plan to de-stress husband Rick

- March 31, 2016—United Airlines flight 326 shot down by a SAM
- April 1, 2016—Meeting in Auletta's office with Buster
- April 1, 2016—Delta flight 219 shot down by a SAM
- April 3, 2016—United Airlines flight 439 shot down a SAM
- April 4—Ellen gets sick
- April 10 —St Mary's school is bombed
- April 12—United flight 301 hit with missile
- April 30—Canadian Pacific train bombing
- May 19—Rick meets with Dr. Buchannan in Washington, then with Barbara Auletta
- May 20—Rick visits Ellen
- May 21—Cruise Ship *Ocean Ecstasy* sets sail
- May 25—The raid on the factory in Baltimore
- May 30—Rick goes to Washington to meet Amanda Reynolds.

Nothing in your style sheet is for the public or your readers. It's for you and your editor. The time it takes you to create a style sheet will save time down the road, and it will be easier to write your next book, especially if it's the next novel in a series. Always keep the style sheet document open while you're writing. I keep the style sheet, cast of characters (which *will* be in the book), and chapter outline open.

If you hire an editor, and you should, a style sheet is essential. The editor will create one if you don't provide it, and it will cost you.

Chapter 7

Traditional Publishing or Self-Publishing

The Revolution in the Publishing Industry

Traditional publishing means finding a publisher to buy your book and publish it in exchange for paying you royalties on the sales (and maybe an advance payment against future royalties). The publisher owns all rights to the book and takes all risks. Until a few short years ago, this was the only way that books got published. Vanity or subsidy publishing is becoming extinct, and it should. Basically, it means that you pay somebody to publish your book and they retain significant rights. It was a precursor to self-publishing. You would go to a vanity press with your manuscript, pay a few thousand dollars and voilà, your book is published, resulting in a few hundred books in your garage. True self-publishing, using a new process called *one-off publishing*, is a far better way to get your book out there.

The State of the Publishing Industry, Including Self-Published Books

The number of new books published each year in the U.S. has exploded by more than 600,000 since 2007, to well over 1 million annually. Bowker is the official company recognized by the federal government for issuing an ISBN, the International Standard Book Number. According to a Bowker Report (October 11, 2017), A total of 786,935 books were self-published in 2016, an incredible increase of 375 percent over 2010. And the number of traditionally published books had climbed to over 300,000 by 2013.

According to the authoritative *Publishers Weekly*, unit sales of print books rose 3% in the first half of 2017, compared to the first half of 2016. Books sold from January to June 2017 totaled 310.7 million, up from 302.8 million during the same time period in 2016. The largest increase was in juvenile fiction (up 5%) and juvenile nonfiction (up 4%). Sales in the adult segments increased, but were less robust. Adult nonfiction unit sales went up 2% over the first half of 2016, while adult fiction sales rose just under 1%.

But the publishing industry is having its troubles. In the U.S., publishing company sales peaked in 2007 and have either fallen or remained level in subsequent years, according to reports of the Association of American Publishers (AAP). That's sales, not the number of books published. Similarly, despite a 2.5% increase in 2015, U.S. bookstore sales are down 37% from their peak in 2007, according to the Census Bureau (Publishers Weekly, February 26, 2016). Just a few years ago, a bookstore appeared in almost every village or hamlet. In a shopping center, you would see two or three. No more. Besides Barnes and Noble, many chain bookstores are no longer in existence. Buying a book online from Amazon is simple—with one click. If you pay to subscribe to Amazon Prime, you can get your book in one day. And you save the gas money driving to one of the few remaining brick-and-mortar bookstores. But people, like me, miss the pleasure of browsing a book store.

Despite the early growth of ebooks or electronic books, like the Kindle or Nook, ebook sales are shrinking. After skyrocketing from 2008 to 2012, ebook sales leveled off in 2013 and have fallen more than 10% since then, according to the AAP StatShot Annual 2015. The number of books published has grown dramatically in the past few years, but sales have shrunk.

If you're a self-published author, don't plan on seeing your novel in a bookstore unless the manager is a friend of yours. For every foot of shelf space in a bookstore, there are millions of titles competing for those precious inches. Every book competes with more than thirteen million titles available, both new and those that have been around for a few years. That's a lot of books, and not much shelf-space. If you are lucky enough to wind up in a bookstore, your book will be displayed spine out, not front cover out. You will need to have a dynamite title if you expect a shopper to pick it off the shelf.

A marketing dollar spent today won't go nearly as far as it went just a few years ago.

The large publishers once paid high advances and would also fund book tours and other marketing efforts on behalf of their authors. That is largely a bygone time, except for established authors or celebrities like former presidents. A friend of mine who published a popular nonfiction book in the 1980s, told me about being met at the airport by a limousine, which took him to a luxury hotel to prepare for a few evenings of book signings. Those were the days! Even the big publishers now expect most of the marketing effort to be expended by the author herself. If you're James Patterson, Nelson DeMille, J.K. Rowling, or Stephen King, you get to call a lot of the shots, because publishers know that your books will sell. If your book gets a deal from a medium to small publisher, don't expect bus fare for your book tour.

Cheer Up – Writing fiction is still a joy

It's no exaggeration to say that there has been a revolution in publishing in the past few years, and there is some good news for Indies. The old stigma of self-publishing no longer exists. "2014 ended up being the year the stigma of self-publishing died," according to Hugh C. Howey.

Hugh Howey is a hero of the self-publishing profession. His first series of novels, actually novellas (short novels – More on this later in the book), was the *Wool* series, dystopian tales of a post-apocalyptic earth in the distant future, when mankind lives in gigantic underground silos. He decided to forgo a deal with a small publishing house and set out on his own into self-publishing. He published the first book of the *Wool* series as a Kindle ebook for $.99 in July 2011. At that time, he didn't intend to make it into a series. He wrote *Wool* while working a full-time job. By October, he noticed that the book had taken off, and would sell 1,000 by month's end. He stopped writing another book he was working on and began to churn out other installments of *Wool*. That was a good idea. He released the *Wool Omnibus*, consisting of five installments, in January of 2012. By that summer, he was selling between 20,000 and 30,000 digital books a month, bringing him a monthly income over $150,000.

He quit his day job.

Howey's success is good news for all self-published authors. He contracted with an agent who approached publishing giant Simon & Schuster. The result was a hybrid arrangement that was an industry first. Simon & Schuster offered him a high six-figure deal and allowed him to retain the digital rights. So, he receiveda huge advance, a percentage of hardcover and paperback sales, and got to keep his ebook royalties.

I've read Howey's books, and I say without hesitating, that he has a secret—he's a gifted writer, as good as you'll find. So, don't think you can pen a short book, charge $.99 on Kindle and rake in the money. Maybe you can, but your first job is to write an excellent book, as Howey did.

Don't Stigmatize Yourself

The reason there ever was a stigma behind self-published books was the difference between a self-published book and one published traditionally—the editing was terrible in the self-published book. Some Indie books appeared to be first drafts, with grammatical errors, typos, wooden characters, and confused plots. Writers are starting to get the message as the self-publishing movement matures. If you put out garbage, you'll get garbage reviews, and you will gather no followers wanting to read your next book. The book you're reading will help you write the best book you can, but the job is on your shoulders. Remember Stephen king's words, *"it is possible, with* **lots of hard work, dedication, and timely help,** *to make a good writer out of a merely competent one."*

Back to the Big Choice – Traditional or Self-Publish

Traditional publishing means that you must find a publisher to buy your book. To say that it's easier said than done is an understatement. To get a large publishing house to even *look* at your book, you will first have to land an agent, who will take a well-earned percentage off the top, usually 15 percent. No law requires you to go through an agent, but don't bother to try it yourself unless you're targeting small publishing companies. Many publishers advertise on their websites that they only accept queries from agents. Small publishing companies will often take on a non-agented author, and a few even advertise that fact.

Agents act as gatekeepers for the publishing companies, to separate the (subjective) garbage from the worthwhile. These folks are just trying to make an honest buck, but they know that the way to earn it is to engender the trust of the publishers to whom they pitch. To find an agent willing to represent you, first you must engage in a time-consuming and emotionally draining process called querying. You make your pitch to agents by sending query letters, which are sales letters, promoting your book and yourself. You could fill a library with books on how to write the perfect query letter. I recommend that you subscribe to *Writer's Digest* and read what they have to say. *Writer's Digest Tutorials* also have video courses on writing query letters. You will then begin your collection of rejection letters, usually by email these days. Back when I was pitching agents a few years ago I received a rejection that I'll never forget. I got the reply by email less than 30 seconds after I hit send. The letter contained the usual boilerplate drivel: "We have reviewed your proposal, and while you obviously have talent, you're not the right fit for us at this time." I doubt that the autoresponder software read my manuscript in 30 seconds. Agents read so much bullshit that they're not afraid to shovel some of it back. Keep in mind, and this is important, that you are sending queries into an arena with the fierce competition numbers I discussed above.

Agents receive hundreds of queries a day, and if you find one willing to do business with you, the agent then pitches the acquisition editors at the publishing companies, who also receive hundreds of queries a day. If you haven't noticed already, the field is not just crowded; it's glutted.

Once your agent finds a publisher willing to buy your book, you may be looking at a two-year time horizon before the thing gets published. The publisher will give you a five percent royalty—and most of the marketing will be done by you. There's little joy in any of this crap.

Does your age have anything to do with an agent's selecting you? No agent will admit it, of course, but look at life from her point of view. An agent hopes that you will write more books and become part of her family of authors. If you're young or middle age, consider giving traditional publishing a shot. You have nothing to lose except time, and a few hairs that you're likely to pull out. If you're, say, 65 years old, the agent will wonder how many more books you've got in you. So, go ahead and call a cop, but no agent will admit to age discrimination.

The Publishing World is Subjective

One reader will write a breathless review, praising you and your book as brilliant parts of the literary universe. Another may find both you and your book to be garbage. A great website to check out is www.litrejections.com. As the name implies, it's all about rejections, famous ones. Let's look at a few stories that are listed on the site. Be prepared to laugh - and to be motivated.

- Louis L'Amour – 200 rejections before Bantam picked him up. He's now their top gun, having sold 330 million books.

- Dr. Seuss – "Too different from other juveniles on the market to warrant its selling," according to one of his rejection letters. He's sold over 300 million books and is the ninth best-selling fiction authors of all time. "Too different," indeed.

- Zane Gray – "You have no business being a writer and should give up." Gray ignored that advice, didn't give up, and went on to sell over 250 million books.

- Jack Canfield and Mark Victor Hansen – "Anthologies don't sell." But *Chicken Soup for the Soul* sold over 125 million copies.

- C.S. Lewis – *The Chronicles of Narnia* sold over 100 million copies after he went through years of rejection.

- Jacqueline Susann – "Undisciplined, rambling and thoroughly amateurish writer," said one rejection letter. But she hung in there, and *The Valley of the Dolls* racked up sales of 30 million copies.

- William P. Young – After 20 rejections Young decided to self-publish *The Shack*, which sold 15 million copies.

And I should remind you that J.K. Rowling, author of the famed Harry Potter series, saw her first book, *Harry Potter and the Philosopher's Stone,* turned down by 12 publishing houses. The Harry Potter series has sold more than 500 million copies, making them the best-selling books in history. Ms. Rowling went on to become the first billionaire author. As I said, the world of publishing is a world of subjectivity.

So, after you've read all my concerns about traditional publishing, why would any unknown writer seek a big company publishing deal? Beats me. I like to play the odds, and the odds are stacked against you and me with the big kahunas. So, let's look at self-publishing.

"One-Off Publishing" sparked the revolution, aided by electronic book publishing. *One-off* simply means that the one-off press cranks out a book when it is ordered, obviating the need for a press run of thousands of books. The technology amazes me—think of a vending machine. The one-off publisher puts in an edited manuscript, and out pops a book. Some of the big names in the field are Author House, iUniverse, Xlibris, Ingram Spark and Createspace, which is owned by Amazon and recently merged with Kindle Direct Publising (KDP). I have published 16 novels and two paperback nonfiction books through Createspace, and will soon see my first paperback with KDP. Every one of my books is on Kindle.

A Big Decision - Go Wide, or Go with Amazon KDP

Should you give Amazon an exclusive right (every 90 days) to sell your books, or should you "go wide," and distribute through a company like Smashwords or Draft2Digital. If you go with one of those companies, your book will be available on a lot of platforms, including iBooks (Apple), Barnes and Noble, Kobo, and others.

At a first glance, it seems to make sense to go wide, publishing your book on multiple platforms. Not so fast. Amazon isn't a 10-foot gorilla, it's a 100-foot gorilla. And the gorilla wants to make you happy by giving you special deals if your go with the KDP platform.

Enrolling in KOLL and Kindle Unlimited

To make your book available in both the Kindle Online Lending Library (KOLL) and Kindle Unlimited (KU), you need to enroll in KDP Select.

KOLL is Amazon's online ebook-lending library. Anyone with a Kindle device can borrow up to one ebook per calendar month at no charge. KU is Amazon's ebook subscription service, which allows readers to pay a flat monthly rate to read as many ebooks as they like. If a reader signs up for Kindle Unlimited for $9.99 per month, they can download a Kindle book for free from any author who has enrolled in KDP.

All my books are on Kindle, for which Amazon pays a 70 percent royalty if I price the Kindle book at $2.99 or higher (known as the "sweet spot."). Less than that and your royalty is 35 percent. You can upload your book on the KDP site (Kindle Direct Publishing) yourself, and it's not that complicated. As I said earlier, you should publish electronically *and* on paper. Your royalties are paid within sixty days by direct deposit to your bank account.

So, I can self-publish my book and get a 70 percent royalty or try to land a big publishing house through an agent, wait for a couple of years and settle for five percent, even though I have to do the marketing myself.

A word about "luck." I've discussed the travails you will need to go through to get noticed by an agent and then a publisher. Sometimes a book deal gets done at a cocktail party to which you were fortunate enough to be invited. At the party, you meet an acquisitions editor of a big publishing house and you two hit it off. Your manuscript lands on his desk because, after a few drinks, he encouraged you to send it to him. Life isn't always fair. Sometimes it depends on luck.

A New Way of Getting Paid

Amazon has figured out a way to compensate an author even if nobody buys her book. The author must enroll in the KDP Select program to get these royalties. Two programs enable this, Kindle Unlimited and the KOLL (Kindle Owner's Lending Library) from Amazon Prime. The two are often confused. In the Kindle Unlimited program, a reader pays $9.99 per month and can pick from over 1.5 million books that can be downloaded for free. A member is allowed to have a maximum of 10 books at any one time. There is no time limit to how long you can keep a book, but if you want to download more than 10, you must "return" a book to get another one. The other program is Amazon Prime, which costs $99 per year. Part of the Prime membership includes the KOLL (Kindle Owner's Lending Library). To borrow a book, you must own a Kindle device. It will not work with a Kindle app on your iPhone or iPad. KOLL allows a reader to borrow one book a month free. In the KOLL program, an author is paid a flat royalty per borrow, and it varies each month depending on the size of the fund that is created with the membership fees. So, a reader gets your book for nothing. Bad idea? Amazon will pay you, even if the customer hasn't laid out any money. It sounds creepy, but Amazon tracks the number of pages that people read in your ebook. It's called the Kindle Edition Normalized Page (KENP). The royalty is roughly $.0045, about half a penny a page. It varies month to month. If your readers go through 1000 pages per day, that yields an estimated $4.50 per day (multiply 1000 pages read by 00.45). 10,000 pages a day gets you $45 a day. Do the math. Last month (September, 2018) my readers read 218, 481 pages of my books. That translates into about $983 in KENP royalties. It's a pioneering way to compensate an author. To get in on this you, the author, must enroll in the Kindle Direct Publishing program (KDP), which costs nothing. The only downside to the Kindle Direct Publishing program is that you give Amazon the exclusive right to sell your work online. For my first book, I chose *not* to give Amazon an exclusive. After a year, I had sold over 10,000 books with Amazon, and three—yes, THREE—books on the other site. And, if you're not exclusive to Amazon, you don't get in on the pages read deal (KENP). Amazon gets the money to pay the pages-read royalties from its membership fees. In case you haven't noticed, Jeff Bezos is a genius. That's probably why he's the richest man in the world.

Self-publishing novels is a joy. But first, you must write the book. If you think I'm being a tedious nudge, I don't care. If you want to publish a book, you first need to write the friggin thing.

Chapter 8

Some Essential Things You Should Do

As I mentioned earlier in this book, I've been writing most of my life, mainly as a legal journalist, so I had a few basics down, like punctuation and grammar. But if you've never written fiction before, I suggest that you consider a few things that I've found useful, and in some cases essential. Writing fiction is different from writing nonfiction, and it's not just a question of making things up in fiction.

Buy Your Own ISBN

You should **buy your own ISBN** rather than having your self-publishing company buy it for you. The benefit of doing this is that you will be listed in the book as the publisher. You may want to create your own imprint, as I did with the name Coddington Press. I'm proud and happy to be an Indie, but I would rather that people see Coddington Press as my publisher, rather than KDP or Ingram Spark. Some of the big players in the self-publishing business, like iUniverse, Xlibris, and Author House will not allow you to supply your own ISBN, thereby insuring that they will forever be known as your publisher. One ISBN will cost you $125. I always buy them in groups of ten which, as of this writing, costs $295, which means that this is the way to go. You assign one ISBN for your paperback, one for your ebook (although it's not required for an ebook), and one for your audiobook.

As I began my first novel, I was hit with a jarring thought: I didn't know anything about writing fiction. Of course, I had a few basic ideas, such as putting quotation marks around a character's words in dialog. But that was about it, other than the things I knew subliminally from reading novels; like there should be a hero, and the hero should do good and interesting stuff. So, as I wrote my first novel, I simultaneously began to educate myself on the craft of writing fiction. The following suggestions are mine, and I'm sure a lot of other good ideas are floating around that I haven't thought of—or tried. The following isn't a hierarchical list of what's most important. They're all important.

• **Writer's Digest.** If *Foreign Affairs* is must-reading for diplomats, *Writer's Digest* is a gotta-have for writers. At eight issues per year, you get a steady source of ideas, advice, inspiration, and challenges to spark your writing career. Serious advice from serious writers on an inexhaustible range of topics. A recent issue is called The Creativity Issue. One of the articles concerned how to generate killer metaphors. I put it to work immediately on a novel I was writing. At $19.96 per year (the cost of lunch at a cheap diner) it's beyond a bargain; it's a simple must.

• **Writer's Digest Tutorials.** Of course, *Writer's Digest* wants to sell you all kinds of additional products, and if it's good, I'm buying. At $199 per year for *Writer's Digest Tutorials*,

I think this subscription is more than worth it. I recommend these tutorials to any writer, new or experienced. At of this writing, there are more than 350 *Writers Digest* tutorials ranging from a half-hour to over an hour. You pour yourself a cup of coffee, sit in front of your computer screen, and listen to a lecture by a highly qualified writing pro. As new courses are added, you're given access to them immediately. Here are some of the current offerings: https://tutorials.writersdigest.com/

- Point of View, parts 1 and 2. Should the narrator of the story be one of the characters in the book (first person POV), or should it be told in the third person?
- Bring your fiction to life
- How to write and sell your memoir
- A guide to drafting the best query letter (If you're looking for a traditional publishing contract)
- Writing and querying the Romance Novel, parts 1 and 2
- Create Edge-of-Your-Seat Suspense: Increase tension by getting into your reader's heads
- Writing Dialog: Bring Your Character's Words to Life. Parts 1 and 2
- How to Get Your Novel Noticed with Stronger First Pages. Parts 1 and 2
- How to Write Crime Fiction

The list goes on and on. I learned how to write dialog using these tutorials as I began my first novel. You should set aside some time each day to delve into this treasure trove of writing advice. According to *The Atlantic*, the average cost of getting an MFA – Master's in Fine Arts— at one of the top-10 schools, is $38,000 a year. Add in room and board and you're looking at $100,000. (*The Atlantic*—"M.F.A.s: An Increasingly Popular, Increasingly Bad Financial Decision." Dec. 19, 2014). I'd rather spent $199 a year and get a writing education while I'm having coffee in my den.

- **James Patterson Teaches Writing - Master Class** - Don't expect a fully developed course, but it's worth the $97 cost, which enables you to watch his classes over and over again. Master James, in short, digestible videos, discusses everything he knows about writing, which is quite a bit.

- **Write every day**. Even if you're just writing in a journal, keep your writing mojo in high gear by doing this. How about getting a website (which can be quite cheap) and blogging, which is nothing more than writing articles for the Internet? Check out www.wix.com, a terrific site for creating your own website, with easy-to-follow instructions. Some writers swear that regular blogging is the best form of marketing. Gather fans, and you have an email list of people who may be future customers for your books. Also, check out www.blogger.com and www.wordpress.com. Not a day goes by that I don't see a message in my inbox about the splendors of blogging. But just like writing a book, make sure your blog posts are well written and provide real value for the reader.

I always have at least three books cooking at various stages of completion. My latest novel, *The Maltese Incident,* a time travel adventure, was published in June of 2018. Then comes *Leonardo*

Murphy, a book about a precocious, 12-year-old. Next on deck is *A Violent Sea*, sequel to *The Maltese Incident. The Violent Sea* has been picked up by a medium sized publisher. In a year or so I intend to revise the book you're reading to share my experience with traditional publishing. I've begun work on *A Sea of Fear*, which will be the sequel to *The Violent Sea.*

Why do I work so hard? It's not work; it's magic.

• **Discipline your muse** to work for you, not the other way around. A muse is a source of inspiration for a creative artist. I think the word muse (from Greek and Roman mythology) was created by some goof-off. Writer friends who tell me that they write when the "muse hits them," are, if you'll pardon my Greek, full of shit. I do love the idea behind the muse—a mysterious source of inspiration—but you must recognize that the muse is *in you* and it shouldn't show up when *it* wants to, but rather when you want it to. Summon the damn thing when you sit down at the keyboard. As the great novelist, Jack London, said: "You can't wait for inspiration. You have to go after it with a club."

I promise you this: When you start to write, the muse just shows up. No kidding; that's how it works.

• **Writer's block does not exist.** Just start writing— Drill this into your consciousness. Maybe put it on a post-it note® on the side of your computer. The concept of writer's block was invented by the same jerk who writes when his muse visits him. Sure, there are times when I look at the screen, and nothing shows up in my mind. So what? I just start writing—

not gibberish, but something to do with the story. Sometimes, I take five minutes and write down some fast notes to get my brain working on the story. Do this, and you will find that the words start to shoot out of your fingertips. I promise—it happens. But you're probably thinking that you can't just put down the words if the words just aren't showing up in your mind. Just start writing something, something relevant to your story, even if it's dumb and doesn't fit. That's the function of rewriting.

• **What to do when your story is stuck**. Being stuck is not the same as writer's block (which does not exist, remember?). You get stuck when the story suddenly stops and you're not sure where to go, and your characters aren't helping you. This seldom happens to a strict outliner, but often occurs with pansters or in-betweeners (like me). The story suddenly doesn't seem to be going anywhere, and you're not sure where it should go. You have a general structure in mind, but you can't see what's next. My suggestion is to let the draft sit for a few days or weeks. It does not make any sense to keep writing at this stage because even though dialog seems to flow, the end isn't anywhere in sight. As I suggest throughout this book, it's a good idea to have a few writing projects at various stages of development. Go to one of your other projects. Your characters will be happy when you return to them.

• **Set aside a definite time to write**. I'm not advocating this, but I put it here for you to consider because it's gospel to many writers. If you have a full-time job, this step is probably essential. Some people write in the early morning, some late at night. I'm retired from my old business as a legal journalist and publisher, and I'm free to set my own hours. Sometimes I write in the morning, sometimes in the afternoon or evening. It depends on other commitments that show up in my life. Would I skip the funeral of my good friend's mother just because I have a rule to write in the morning? Rather than saddle myself with a rule I may have to break, I plan my writing time each day. Totally up to you. Many writers, perhaps most, insist on writing at the same time each day. Not me. Your call. So, here's the rule—be flexible.

Some good books on writing:

- *On Writing: A Memoir of the Craft* by Stephen King. Words from a master. I keep reading this book over and over. Don't think about it; just get this book. You can borrow it from a library if you're on a tight budget, but you can't mark it up as if it's your own. If you are serious about writing, this book belongs in your professional library, and its words belong in your brain. I recommend getting it in hardcover or paperback rather than as an ebook because then you can dog-ear and scribble notes in the margin. If you own a Kindle device or have downloaded the app onto your cell phone or iPad you can hit a key and insert notes. As always, do what works best for you. I also bought *On Writing* as an audiobook. Stephen King himself narrated the book, and he did an excellent job. Something about hearing the words of a master from his own lips as I'm emptying the dishwasher just does it for me.

- *The Writer's Primer: A Practical Guide for Aspiring Authors Seeking Publication* by Roland Allnach. The subheading says this book is a primer, but it covers the waterfront of the basics of becoming an author. Roland Allnach, an award-winning writer, goes into some well-researched detail on the differences, including the pluses and minuses, of traditional publishing, small press publishing, and self-publishing. There are no subjects on the matter of becoming an author that Allnach doesn't treat in detail, from the writing itself to the necessary subject of marketing. If you're new to the craft of writing or even if you have published more than one book, this volume belongs on your bookshelf. The book you're reading, as you can see, concentrates mainly on writing. Allnach's book shows you everything you will encounter as you start your writing career.

- *The War of Art: Break through the Blocks and Win Your Inner Creative Battles* by Steven Pressfield. Every field of endeavor needs a source of motivation and inspiration. On the subject of writing inspiration, this book does just that. Pressfield is famous for his novel, *The Legend of Bagger Vance,* as well as many other novels, screenplays, and non-fiction works. Word-playing on the title of the Sun Tzu classic *The Art of War,* this book is about the war that an artist wages with himself, a war against resistance, whether it's procrastination, failing to start a project, or a stubborn refusal (not conscious by the way) to get your work done. I bought this as an audiobook, and I recommend it for its excellent narrative by Shawn Coyle. Just as I constantly read or listen to Stephen King's *On Writing*, I keep listening to *The War of Art*. I find it especially useful when returning from a book signing where I sold only a few books. Disappointment and discouragement come with the profession of writing. This book is the perfect antidote.

- *The Chicago Manual of Style* (16 Edition). THE informative source of the written word in American English. This is not a book that you read. It's strictly for reference. If you choose to read it cover to cover, rest assured that you are a boring person.

- *The Transitive Vampire*, by Karen Elisabeth Gordon. Books on grammar should be entertaining and funny; otherwise they won't get read. This book fits the bill. She inserts old artwork at the beginning of each chapter and writes hysterical captions.

- *Eats, Shoots and Leaves* by Lynne Truss. As funny as *The Transitive Vampire* and equally important. This book takes on bad punctuation. Lynne Truss, a self-appointed grouch, gets the title of her book from an encyclopedia entry about pandas. Under the subject of the panda's eating habits, the bozo who wrote the entry inserted a comma after the word "eats," leaving the reader to envision a panda shooting a gun and leaving after it eats.

Thus, "eats, shoots and leaves," rather than eats shoots and leaves.

- *The Elements of Style*, 4th Edition. Strunk and White. First written by William Strunk in 1918 and updated by E.B. White, this book still sells like crazy—it ranks 146 overall on Amazon. At 105 pages, this is a book you should read. Timeless advice, well, mostly timeless. The book is commonly referred to not by its title but by its authors, Strunk and White. Strunk insists you should never begin a sentence with "however," but the reading and writing public has ignored this (I agree with Strunk). The book also urges you to eliminate useless words. That advice alone is worth the small price you pay for the book. They also emphasize that you should use the active voice, not passive, critically important advice.

- **Join a Writers Group**. Nothing complicated about a writers group. It's an organization of writers and would-be writers who meet regularly and offer advice to each other. Some groups organize critiquing sessions, where the members offer opinions on another member's work. Many groups actively seek out book-signing opportunities. Just like a Rotary Club or a Chamber of Commerce, the value of belonging to such a group depends on the dedication of its members, and whether you enjoy their company. If you find yourself in a group that doesn't bring value to your writing career, you should leave the group and spend the time working on your next novel. I belong to an organization called the

Long Island Authors Group (LIAG). I find real value in my membership as well as the benefit of meeting with friends.

- **Attend Writer's Conferences**. Listen to speakers, share ideas, meet new people, and maybe have fun. I'm not a big fan of writer's conferences, but that doesn't mean that you should avoid them (like I do). I once attended a conference where each of us was given an assignment to write 200 words based on the something we each saw in a nearby art exhibit. This is the idea of writing based on a prompt. My eyes lit upon a framed beam section from the World Trade Center attack. The thought crossed my mind that the beam might have once been located hundreds of feet in the sky. For me, it sparked my fear of heights, so I wrote 200 words on that subject. My critique "partner" was totally exercised that I used the first personal pronoun throughout the short piece. She dropped not-so-subtle hints that I may have a problem with my egocentric writing. How I could write about *my* problem with height without referring to myself is a question that went unanswered. A complete waste of time. Your call. If it works, keep doing it, if not, save your money and get back to the keyboard.

Chapter 9

Some Basics of Any Novel

Start with a compelling opening

Pay careful attention to your first few pages, especially the first page, and even the first sentence. Think of yourself as a reader. An exciting opening makes you want to read further, as simple as that. Whenever I'm asked to talk to a school group about reading or writing, I always begin with a challenge: "Read the first few pages of *Jaws* by Peter Benchley, and then stop reading if you can." I use the first chapter of *Jaws* to ignite the reading fire within high schoolers. The story begins with a young woman who decides to take a late-night swim. Her boyfriend is asleep on the beach, having partied too much. Here is an excerpt from the first chapter of *Jaws*:

"The fish smelled her now, and the vibrations—erratic and sharp—signaled distress. The fish began to circle close to the surface. Its dorsal fin broke water, and its tail, thrashing back and forth, cut the glassy surface with a hiss. A series of tremors shook its body.

"For the first time, the woman felt fear, though she did not know why. Adrenaline shot through her trunk and her limbs, generating a tingling heat and urging her to swim faster. She guessed that she was fifty yards from shore. She could see the line of white foam where the waves broke on the beach. She saw the lights in the house, and for a comforting moment, she thought she saw someone pass by one of the windows.

"The fish was about forty feet from the woman, off to the side, when it turned suddenly to the left, dropped entirely below the surface, and, with two quick thrusts of its tail, was upon her.

"At first, the woman thought she had snagged her leg on a rock or a piece of floating wood. There was no initial pain, only one violent tug on her right leg. She reached down to touch her foot, treading water with her left leg to keep her head up, feeling in the blackness with her left hand. She could not find her foot. She reached higher on her leg, and then she was overcome by a rush of nausea and dizziness. Her groping fingers had found a hub of bone and tattered flesh. She knew that the warm, pulsing flow over her fingers in the chill water was her own blood." *Jaws*, by Peter Benchley, latest edition published July 31, 2012, Random House.

You're going to put the book down, right? As I challenge kids, I challenge you. If you have not read the book already, try to stop reading *Jaws* after what you've just read. No pun intended on the word fish, but you're hooked.

Another one of my favorite openings is Karen Thompson Walker's *The Age of Miracles*, a lovely coming-of-age tale about a young girl's experience when disaster strikes from a slowing of the earth's rotation. Here are the opening lines that made me buy the book:

"We didn't notice right away. We couldn't feel it.

We did not sense at first the extra time bulging from the smooth edge of each daylike a tumor blooming beneath the skin."

Put that book back on the shelf? I don't think so.

More than a few people have told me that the first page of my book, *The Skies of Time*, pushed them into reading further. Here it is:

"Are you ready, honey?"

"Honey? Hey, Ashley, you're an admiral. Aren't you supposed to call me 'lieutenant' or something?"

"You're my husband, dammit, and I'll call you whatever I want—honey."

"Aye aye, sweetheart."

A flight crewman hooked the launch bar on my F/A-18 F Super Hornet's nose gear to the catapult shuttle. The catapult officer gave the launch signal to the operator sitting in his "cat house," the control pod that's recessed into the flight deck. He opened a valve to fill the catapult's cylinder with high-pressure steam. On a signal from one of the flight crew, I eased the throttle forward to full power, and then signaled that I was ready to launch. The catapult operator released the pistons, causing a "holdback" to drop away, and we shot off the deck of the USS *Abraham Lincoln* at a speed of 165 miles per hour. I felt the same exhilaration as I did the first time I took off from a carrier deck, a feeling that's never left me.

"How was that, hon?" I asked, as we gained speed and altitude.

"Well, I'm still holding in my breakfast, if that's what you mean."

"Any regrets about our flight so far, Jack?"

"Yeah, I regret that I married such a boring woman."

"No problem, babe, I can fix that."

I looked to see if we were beyond sight of the carrier and told my escorts to fall back. I pulled back and put the nose of the Hornet into a vertical climb. I heard Jack say,

"Oh, my God!" *The Skies of Time*, by Russell F. Moran, Coddington Press, 2015.

The idea behind a compelling first page is simple—to convince the reader to turn the page to see what's next. It's a concept similar to good copywriting. What is the purpose of the first line of an advertisement? To get the reader to read the second line. What is the purpose of the second line? To get the reader to the third line. You get the idea. You must lead your reader from one line to the next. That's why we buy so much shiny stuff we don't need. An excellent book on copywriting is *The Adweek Copywriting Handbook* by Joseph Sugarman. As I discuss later, your marketing efforts for your book will require you to become skilled in copywriting, especially when you write your book's description that will appear on Amazon.

Backstory – Handle with Care

"Backstory" means filling in the reader on what happened before, maybe in a previous book in a series. Or it can mean just telling (ouch – telling?) the reader about some character or an event that happened before. You may also find it useful to explain something in the past even if you haven't written about it before, just to set the table for the unfolding story.

You can kill the flow of your novel by dumping in a few paragraphs because you think that you must. Sometimes, quite often, you do need to bring the reader up to speed. But if it's just a big word dump, where you tell without showing, it can damage your story.

Perhaps the best way to handle backstory is to dribble it in over a few chapters. You will often do this in dialog, or, if writing in the first person, the narrator does the talking.

"I'll never forget our wedding day." The reader will tense up, expecting a backstory word dump. But if you make a few comments about the wedding day, assuming it's important, do it in a few scenes, preferably in dialog.

"I'll never forget our wedding day," Jim said, as he poured Harry another beer.

"I've noticed that Jane just rolled her eyes any time your wedding day came up in conversation," Harry said.

"It was a great wedding until the drunk from hell took out a pistol and shot the band leader. The guy's still in prison."

Jim had to introduce this backstory because, later in the book, the drunk from hell gets out of jail and brings chaos to Jim and Jane's life.

Backstory is often needed if there was a prequel to the book you're writing. Just handle it with care and make the backstory a part of your present story, not just a bunch of words with no reason to exist. And remember, dribble it in over a few scenes.

To Be or Not to Be – Watch out for those linking verbs.

The following discussion could also be titled, "Use the active tense where possible."

Linking verbs are words used to describe a *state of being*. The most common linking verb is "to be," and its basic forms such as am, is, are, was, were, be, been, and being. Other linking verbs can also be action words.

Linking – Jenny appeared to be drunk.

Action – Jenny appeared in the doorway.

Linking – He looked to be amused by something.

Action – He looked both ways before crossing the street.

When we write, we naturally need to use both linking and action verbs, because both verb types play a critical role in the English language. But the overuse of linking verbs can make a piece of writing flat. Where possible, don't just tell what something is; *tell what it does.*

Action verbs liven up your writing, giving it some zing. Compare the following two sentences.

"Harry was the tallest man on the bridge." The linking verb "was" describes a state of being tall. How about the following instead?

"Harry towered over the other officers on the bridge."

The action word towered gives the idea more pizzazz than just telling us about Captain Harry's state of being as tall.

Let's look, at a few other examples.

Passive – "Ten soldiers were standing on the dock."

Active – "Ten soldiers stood on the dock."

Passive – "There are two reasons why I'm not going to buy this car."

Active – "I won't buy this car for two reasons."

Passive – "Jenny was walking down the hallway."

Active – "Jenny walked down the Hallway."

My friend and editor, John White, told me a story about an author who, on a dare, wrote a novel without any form of the verb "to be." He deleted any form of the verb from the entire book. A bit extreme, perhaps, but a dare is a dare. I prefer John's approach. Limit your use of "to be" verbs to one per paragraph, and no more than three per page.

Murder Your Darlings

Sir Arthur Quiller-Couch was an English novelist born in 1863, who often wrote under the pseudonym Q. For all his prodigious output, including *The Oxford Book of English Verse*

1250–1900, he's perhaps most famous for his short and punchy advice to novelists: "Murder your darlings."

What is a "darling" and why should you murder it? A darling is a word, phrase, or sentence that you fall in love with because you think it shows people that you are witty and wise. It's so erudite that you want to pat yourself on the back for your brilliance in writing it. Problem is, you wrote it for yourself, not the reader, who thinks that you're just full of shit. Editors are great for spotting darlings. You love your darlings so much you don't pay attention to them on rewrite, except maybe to gloat over your literary talent. Whenever you come across one of these too-cute pieces of writing, ask yourself this question: "Does this work or not?"

Stephen King takes up Quiller-Couch's advice in his book *On Writing*. "Kill your darlings, kill your darlings, even when it breaks your egocentric little scribbler's heart, kill your darlings." Emphasis added. King, Stephen. *On Writing: A Memoir of The Craft* (Kindle Location 2497). Scribner. Kindle Edition.

Always remember, you write for the reader.

Show Don't Tell

You will hear this admonition any time you read about the art of writing fiction. The phrase means what it says. *Show* the reader what is going on in the scene rather than telling or explaining the story. It gives life to what could be a dull narrative. Let's look at a few examples:

Tell: "She looked lovingly into his eyes."

Show: "She put down her glass, walked up to him and placed her hands on his chest, never once taking her eyes from his."

Tell: "Jack was hot and exhausted after his run."

Show: "Jack grabbed a towel from the table and wiped the sweat that was cascading down his face after his run. He staggered across the floor, his leg muscles throbbing as he looked for a place to sit."

Tell: "Harry was furious."

Show: "Harry's face throbbed beet red as he slammed his briefcase onto the table, knocking the coffee setting to the floor."

Or, as put so eloquently by Anton Checkov, "Don't Tell Me the Moon Is Shining; Show Me the Glint of Light on Broken Glass."

Telling is fine if you're writing an article, an essay, or a nonfiction book. But for fiction, you need to make the reader feel part of the action. The book should disappear, and the story should take its place. Think of a well-done scene from a movie or TV show. A good writer can show you the action even without dialog. The director of the movie, *Dunkirk*, showed us the story amidst bullets, exploding bombs, and most importantly, the looks on the actors' faces. Kenneth Branagh's face carried you to the bloody boat dock as an airplane strafed the soldiers waiting to escape. Imagine if the writer put in a few words for Branagh to speak, like: "I'm really frightened." No, the writers and directors chose to show you the emotion rather than tell you about it. It's useful to think about a movie scene as you're writing. How would you bring your words to the screen? As you go through successive rewrites of your book, be on the lookout for scenes where you can show the reader what's going on, avoiding the strong temptation to tell the story yourself. Trust your characters—they'll do a great job of putting on a show for your reader. It's important to recognize that we all have a deep desire to tell the story to make sure the reader gets it. Trust your readers—they'll get it even if you don't explain it. Just show it to them. We've got to stamp out that desire. If the reader "sees" a woman with her hands on a guy's chest as she stared into his eyes, don't worry—the reader knows she's looking into the man's eyes "lovingly."

Point of View

Point of View or POV is one of those critical choices you must make before you start your novel. Who's telling the story, and whose story is it? Here are the points of view from which you need to choose, and yes, you can change the POV throughout the book:

1. First Person. "I ran the 60-yard dash in 6.7 seconds."

2. Third Person subjective. "He ran the 60-yard dash and was sure he did it under 7 seconds."

3. Third person objective. "He ran the 60-yard dash, and the stopwatch confirmed 6.7 seconds."

4. Third person omniscient. "Everyone gathered around the track, some begrudgingly so because it was a hot,

sticky day. Nancy wondered if she could run the 60-yard dash faster than George." Note that the third person omniscient is able to put in all sorts of cool stuff because, hey, he's omniscient.

In the *Writer's Digest Tutorial* on POV, the narrators are Charlotte Robin Cook and Jon James Miller, both experienced novelists. Charlotte Cook makes an important point at the beginning. In the American market, readers prefer the first person POV. That made me happy because I love to write in the first person. The narrator is telling the story, and using the first person POV enables me to get inside the character's head. In the Third person POVs, a person not present is telling the story. In the omniscient POV, a godlike narrator who knows all is telling the reader what happens, sometimes reaching back over history to provide background. In the first person POV, there is an intimacy and immediacy that you can't find with other POVs. You put yourself inside the mind of the narrator, and describe what's going on, even giving your deep thoughts and opinions. It's a great way to tell a story, because it comes naturally to the writer—she's experiencing what the character is saying.

If you're writing from the first person POV, can there be more than one narrator? Definitely. In a book I'm writing now, a sea captain is attracted to a beautiful passenger, and she's attracted to him. I switch between the two characters as they narrate their own stories, showing you their feelings, doubts, and hopes, each wondering if the other will feel the same way. Later in the book, I also wrote from the point of view of a CIA agent in the first person. CAUTION: The most important thing to keep in mind, no matter what point of view you're writing in, is that the reader MUST KNOW who's talking. My rule is always to identify the narrator in the first sentence. You don't need to say, "This is Captain Harry speaking," but rather any identifying words such as, "Marrying Meg was the best thing I've ever done." The reader knows that Harry and Meg got married, so that sentence tells you Captain Harry is talking. If my CIA guy is speaking, I'll begin a chapter with something like: "They call me Buster because I can be a ball buster at times." It's easy to do, just make sure you don't confuse the reader.

Can you mix first and third person POVs in the same story? Yes, again make sure the reader knows what's going on. In one chapter of my book, *The Maltese Incident*, a ship on the other side of the world is casting off its lines and setting out to sea. I dropped into omniscient third person mode, having fun showing the reader the sights and sounds aboard a cruise ship as it glided down the Hudson River, with Frank Sinatra singing "New York, New York," in the background. It was an experience I had myself a few times. In the book, none of my first-person narrators knew anything about this ship leaving its dock, so the third-person narration was necessary, with the third-person omniscient enlivening the scene a bit.

Where Do You Get Your Ideas?

People ask me this all the time, as they do all writers. I take it as a compliment. If they didn't care for the book, why should they care how I came up with the story to begin with? A classic way to generate ideas is to observe the world around you. Earlier I discussed an incident where Stephen King slipped on a hill and almost fell into a fast-moving river. That occurrence resulted in the book, *From a Buick Eight*. The embankment was a PROMPT, something that got King's creative juices flowing.

In the 2012 movie, *The Magic of Belle Isle*, Morgan Freeman plays an alcoholic, disabled writer who befriends a neighbor and her kids. In a terrific scene that rings true with any writer, Freeman points toward a tree-lined path and asks the little girl what she sees. He guides her to the understanding that the path was a writer's prompt, and that the writer's job is to populate the visual reality with the magic of a story. The screenwriters did a great job with this movie. My favorite scene had Morgan Freeman dreaming about his pretty neighbor (Virginia Madsen). As he bent over to kiss her in his dream, his Labrador Retriever awakens him by slurping his lips. Great flick, and a great job of showing, not telling.

Prompts surround us. A simple scene, such as falling down an embankment, or seeing a tree-lined path, can be just slices of your life, or they can be inspirations for your writing. Your dog pees on the rug, a neighbor backs into your new car, the garbage man throws an empty can on your carefully coddled tomato plant, you wake up to a fire engine's siren. With every issue of *Writer's Digest*, there is a section on writer's prompts.

Try this. When something grabs your attention, and it may be something trivial, drop into improv mode and ask, "What if…?"

Sometimes ideas just pop into your head without the aid of a prompt. The idea just shows up. It may be a memory of something good—or bad. It may be something that comes out of nowhere. Whatever the thought is, see if you can slap a "What if" on it. And don't forget to write it down. I've often thought, "Hey, that's a great idea for a scene." Then, later, when I get back to my keyboard, the idea was no longer in my head. Write it down immediately after the thought goes through your mind.

How Long Should a Novel Be?

Opinions are all over the place on this question, but the most common answer is 50,000 words. Take that number as a bare minimum to be safe. NaNoWriMo, the National Novel Writing Month people, puts the number at 50,000 words and the challenge is to write that amount in one month (hence, National Novel Writing Month). After that number, things start to get weird, and I shall not add to the weirdness. The weirdness advisors say that the ideal page-length of a science fiction novel is one number, a crime novel another, and historical fiction yet a different number of pages. I have never been able to figure out why the numbers change with different genres, nor have I read an intelligible explanation as to why the numbers vary. Yes, for an historic epic that unfolds over generations, you would expect a long book, but beyond that I don't understand where the pundits come up with their numbers. Here are the (arbitrary) numbers for different types of writing. How many words to a page? It varies, of course, but I've found that over 15 novels, the average words per page for my books is 231, and it won't vary too much from there unless a book has little dialog, and therefore not much white space, or a lot of dialog resulting in lots of white space. So, for me, a 50,000-word book translates into about 217 pages.

Here are some numbers that are often agreed upon:

- Novel – 50,000 words

- Novella – 17,500 to 49,999 words

- Novelette (a somewhat derogatory term) - 7,500 to 17,499 words

- Short Story 7,500 words, although some will tell you that the limit is 5,000 words.

- Bottom line – Consider these word counts to be approximate. The word ballpark should serve you.

Although the numbers are arbitrary, you shouldn't write a large book, say 200,000 words or more (866 pages), if you are a budding novelist looking for a traditional publisher. No agent or acquisitions editor will be willing to invest in such a huge book written by a newbie. The more pages, the higher the production costs. And remember, if you're an Indie, you bear the added cost.

Some writers, such as James Patterson, think that the reading public wants shorter books. Who can argue with the world's best-selling author? Patterson has recently launched "Book Shots," which are novella-length books of about 150 pages (34,500 words) selling for five bucks. His theory, and it has a lot going for it, is that people are so busy they hunger for an inexpensive book they can read in an evening. Patterson is also known for writing novels in collaboration with another writer, and that's why my email inbox has an announcement, sometimes two or three, every week, "The new book by James Patterson (and a co-author)." Some people criticize Patterson for these collaborations, but as he explains in his video master class, some of the greatest works of art come from collaborations. Think Gilbert and Sullivan, Rogers and Hammerstein, Lerner and Lowe, or Strunk and White. Abbot and Costello?

Some pundits insist that novels should be long, at least 300 pages. Nonsense. I enjoy reading the books of Indie novelist E.M Foner. His series, *EarthCent Ambassador*, boasts 14 books. Comedy meets science fiction, and the comedy is hilarious. His titles are terrific, such as *Date Night on Union Station* (Union Station being a space station). I bring it up here because all his books are approximately 180 pages, about 41,000 words. That means his books are short, really novellas, like Patterson's Book Shots. They also sell like crazy on Amazon. So Foner broke, and continues to break, the 50,000-word minimum rule. I don't think he cares. Foner has discovered the joy of writing fiction.

A Word on the Current Trend in Novel Writing

As I discussed in the preceding section about the length of novels, I now make a prediction. Well, I'm not sure it's a prediction about something that may show up in the future because it's happening now. Novels are getting shorter, it's as simple as that. Novels (50,000 words) are being supplanted by novellas (17,500 to 49,999 words). Whether it's James Patterson or E.M Foner, works of fiction are simply getting shorter. We seldom see a novelist announce that his book is a novella, maybe because it sounds kind of funky, and not a lot of people know what it is—a short novel. Patterson, a former advertising executive, is a businessman, not only a novelist. I believe he's not only seeing a trend; he's helping to push it. I think he's dead-on accurate when he says that people want a 150-page work of fiction for under five dollars. But caution. Five dollars won't work as a price in one-off publishing for an Indie author. In other words, at that price, it could cost you money to sell a book, and that is insane. With the gigantic print runs for one of Patterson's books, it becomes possible. So, you need to price your book, even if it's somewhat short, at a level that you can make at least a small profit.

Some of the greatest all-time novels are really novellas. Here are just a few: *Animal Farm; Of Mice and Men; The Metamorphosis; The Old Man and the Sea; The Stranger; The Little Prince; Heart of Darkness; A Clockwork Orange; The Time Machine; The Call of the Wild.*

Sometimes your story is simply finished, and to make it longer is word-stuffing. A recent book of mine turned out to be a novella. *The President is Missing* (No relation to a recent book of the same name by James Patterson and Bill Clinton – Mine was published 13 months before theirs) is 32,600 words long and 130 pages, my shortest book to date. It's also one of my best-selling books. I went through 15 drafts and tried to make it longer, but I realized that I would have to stuff it with unnecessary words. So, with this book and its tightly-woven plot, I joined the trend toward shorter novels. I also predict that the definition of novel will change from 50,000 words to a number far less. If you are a new author, I suggest sticking to the current definition of a novel. When you have a few books under your belt you can start to bend the rules. A-list authors can get away with a lot of things. Take Earnest Hemmingway's *The Old Man and the Sea,* one of the all-time great stories. It's also only 128 pages long. The big guys can also get away with doing things in the other direction. Stephen King's 1986 novel, *It,* is 1,184 pages in paperback. A newbie would be advised to make it into a series of three or four books.

Your real competition

No, it's not other writers and their books—it's the enormous amount of leisure-time choices available today. We live in the Golden Age of Television, and it wasn't always golden. Newton Minow, then chairman of the Federal Communications Commission, declared in a famous speech on May 9, 1961, that television was a "vast wasteland." Programs like *The Jack Benny Show, Dennis the Menace, I Love Lucy, Candid Camera,* and *What's My Line* were the typical offerings in 1961. Fun, yes, but they exercised your brain about as much as a dripping faucet. Most TVs at the time were black-and-white with lousy reception. Curling up with a good novel was a real choice back then. As I write elsewhere in this book, the quality of TV dramas and even sitcoms have improved so much that the TV has earned itself a place in the arts, mainly because of excellent screenwriters and directors, not to mention great actors.

The vast wasteland has been replaced by the Golden Age of Television. Now, with the advent of the digital video recorder, you have the option of never missing your favorite shows. "Binge watching" is a phrase that didn't exist a few years ago, but now you can binge on an entire season of episodes from your favorite show. And you're not wasting time by watching them. The plots are intricate and captivating, engaging your brain. The acting and directing are top quality.

Other modern inventions that shout to us for attention include the Internet, email, and, of course, social media, including Facebook, Twitter, Pinterest, and Linkedin, just to name the big players. I've watched people sitting at a counter in a diner, and, while reading a book, tapping on their cell phone every couple of minutes, checking email no doubt. Multitasking—the American way.

So, what's a humble novelist to do? Accept reality for one thing, because reality doesn't give a rat's ass that people are binge-watching *Criminal Minds* reruns or posting on Facebook while they should be reading the book that you slaved over for a year. People still read novels, but there are enormous competing demands for their attention. Expect to see the trend for shorter novels continue. But look at it positively: shorter novels mean you get to write more books.

Chapter 10

Rewriting and Editing

Rewriting and editing are words often used interchangeably, and appropriately so. As you rewrite, you look for scenes or sentences that don't make sense, you find words that should be replaced. You add stuff and subtract. You also find typos, grammatical mistakes, and spelling errors. Some people say that you should go through an editing pass by just looking for errors, and then look for scene-rewriting needs on the next pass. People like that need a vacation. Too much rigid structure can sap the joy out of writing.

Should you hire an editor?

The simple answer is yes, you should, but the real answer isn't that simple. What kind of editor should you hire? The answer is simple—hire a good one. A good editor will see plot holes and make recommendations for plugging them. A good editor is an expert on grammar and punctuation and will pick up things that you missed. A good editor will work with you to make your book the best it can be. But (and I know you've been expecting the "but") a good editor gets paid a lot of money, sometimes in the multiple thousands, and she's worth it. So, here's the complication to the question, "should you hire an editor?" The complication is—**can you afford it?** Say you find a good editor who's been highly recommended and has lots of praise which she smartly posts on her website. She quotes you $3,000, not bad for a good experienced editor. Let's assume that you're self-publishing your book. The statistics tell you that the odds of your book selling a lot are stacked against you. On top of the editor's fee you must add production costs, the cost of a cover designer, and a marketing budget. I could go on for pages about the benefits of hiring a good editor, but what if you simply can't afford it? I am now going to discuss the alternative to hiring an editor, because that is exactly what most self-published writers do. I'm lucky in that my wife Lynda was a professional editor for many years, so my cost is to make nice, empty the dishwasher, and do the laundry occasionally. But she's not my only editor. I also have a good friend who does a great job editing my work. Let's look at some alternatives to paying an editor.

If you can't afford a professional editor - Ask friends to help you by serving as beta readers.

They need not be editors, either professional or amateur. Beta readers are test readers. Ask them to tell you what they like and dislike about your novel. Some will pick up blatant errors. This is a bonus. After I published my first book a friend called me and pointed out that I had ended a chapter with a comma. Not a sentence or a paragraph, but a friggin chapter. What you're looking for is the gut feelings of a reader. You will hear things like:

"I think Jenny uses foul language too much;"

"How could this happen if that happened first?" Comments like this are valuable—your reader friend is pointing something out that doesn't make sense, a plot twist that keeps on twisting. Professional editors do this all the time.

"I don't find the characters to be real. It seems that they're just characters in a book, not real people."

"I think the US Military Academy is West Point, not West Plant."

"The ending was not satisfying."

"The ending was totally unbelievable."

"The beginning of the book didn't pull me forward."

I have a good friend who volunteered to edit my books. He's a retired teacher. Many pundits will tell you never use the services of a retired teacher friend as your editor. Like much well-meaning advice, that is off cue. Although John's not a professional editor, he was a technical writer as well as a teacher. John has a keen editorial eye and an encyclopedic command of the English language. He sees things that I missed after a number of drafts, and even finds mistakes that my wife overlooked. He even can see an extra space that I missed, because I just didn't see it. In one of my recent novels *The Maltese Incident,* a cruise ship gets lost in time (I love time travel) and the crew and passengers decide to build a community on a deserted island, because the ship was running low on fuel and was starting to break down. So, they built a great community of multiple houses and even a hospital—in a prehistoric forest. My friend John raised a question, which didn't occur to me because I was too busy building a town in a jungle. "Where did they get the tools and materials to build a housing community?" John asked. This was such a gaping hole in the story that you could fit a cruise ship through it. And I didn't see it! So, thanks to John, I wrote that the ship once was owned by an eccentric billionaire who was talented with carpentry and wanted to build himself a town on an island he owned in the Bahamas. Just before the man died, he filled the hold of the ship with enough tools, lumber, and other materials to make it possible for my characters to build their town. Saved by an editor!

Software – Editing Programs

Software that suggests editorial changes to your manuscript use some of the tools of artificial intelligence. As of this writing, I haven't found one that I would describe as great, but I do recommend them because, though not great, they're good.

- **Autocrit calls itself** "Manuscript Editing Software for Fiction Writers." In the product description at autocrit.com you see the areas that the software includes: pacing and momentum, dialog, strong writing, word choice, and repetition. The people behind the software say that it's not just an editor but a coach. I've used and still use this program, and I recommend it, especially if you're new to writing fiction. I've been at it for a while, so I skim over some of the program's recommendations, but I'm always impressed by its scope. You get unlimited access to the program for $30 a month.

- **Grammarly** is, as its names suggests, a grammar checker, comparable to a line or copy editor, but not as sweeping in its scope as Autocrit. The premium version (for which you pay) includes a plagiarism detector, which I suppose is useful if you're a crook. I would never dream of plagiarizing someone else's work, nor should you, so I'm not sure this function is a valuable addition. You will notice Grammarly at work as you type emails. The free version pops up recommendations and they're quite useful. The full version, which enables you to copy and paste parts of your manuscript into the program, costs $30 a month, or an annual discounted price of $139.95. But, and this is a big but, you can only paste 100,000 characters, about 60 pages or four megabytes into the program, so you can only do a few chapters at a time. Another problem with the program is that when you paste your Word document into Grammarly, all your formatting is stripped away. So, after you're done with Grammarly's suggested edits, you must edit the thing all over again after you paste it back into Word. The best way to work around this is to keep your Word document open and put the changes directly into it rather than make the changes in the Grammarly document. Again, it's a grammar (and spelling) checker, not a full-blown editing program like Autocrit. Also, Grammarly disables the "add to dictionary" function in

Word. If you wish to subscribe to only one, by all means go with Autocrit, and use the free version of Grammarly which is floating all over the Internet.

Until recently, Microsoft Word suffered from a literacy problem. Whenever I wrote the possessive "its," Word wanted me to change it to the contraction "it's." Also, Word constantly told me to end declarative sentences with a question mark. I've noticed recently that these problems seem to have disappeared. Maybe Microsoft got tired of writers screaming at it.

Revise, revise, revise.

Besides asking friends to beta-read your novel, you can also try to make up for not having a professional editor by going through a lot of drafts. Yes, we writers are the worst editors of our own work, but by carefully editing your book, over and over again, you can catch most errors. See the next chapter, which is all about drafts.

Revising Your Book After It's Published

What if you discover a mistake after your book is published? I've just read a best-selling book by a best-selling author, published by one of the big publishing companies. After I found a couple of mistakes I decided to keep a count of the errors. The book had no fewer than 12 errors, not counting the ones that I missed. And this guy is a famous, best-selling author, and his publisher no doubt assigned a platoon of proof readers and copy editors before publication. The same thing happens with Indies. We make mistakes. I make mistakes. As a great philosopher once said, "Shit happens." Besides mistakes, what if you think of something that would improve the book? Until recent years making post-publishing changes to a book would cost a small fortune. Now it's no problem. The world of **one-off printing** makes post-publishing revisions easy and cheap. You just make your changes to your document, save it with a new draft number, and upload it to your self-publishing company. The same goes for ebooks, except it's even easier.

Chapter 11

All About Drafts — How Many?

The late English poet and novelist, Robert Graves, famously said: "There is no such thing as good writing, only good rewriting." Ernest Hemingway was more blunt: "The first draft of anything is shit."

I once read a blog entry by a writer who, seeking advice from other authors, said: "I love to write, but I hate going back and editing and rewriting. I really can't stand it." My advice to him, although I didn't say it in print (I have an aversion to saying nasty things about fellow writers, even when they're assholes): "Stop writing and take up the saxophone, or poker playing, or raising guppies, or anything, but stop kidding yourself into believing that you're a writer."

Whether you're self-publishing or trying to attract a traditional publisher, either directly or through an agent, you must do the initial editing and rewriting yourself. Sure, if you land a publisher, you will be assigned to an editor, but your chances of landing that publisher are vastly improved if you submit a polished manuscript, free of spelling and grammatical errors, with a plot that makes sense, and a story that's compelling. If you're self-publishing and use an editor, you want to give her a polished manuscript (and don't forget to include the style sheet).

Okay, so how many drafts? I wish I could give you a definitive answer, but it's up to you. A friend of mine who writes terrific thrillers, says that you should go through a minimum of 25 drafts. That's a bit much for me, but I can't say he's wrong. I put my novels through at least 15 drafts, usually 20, not counting the rounds that my wife or my friend John go through. Unlike the guy who wrote that blog post saying how much he hated rewriting, I enjoy it. I like it because I see in front of my eyes how the story improves with each draft.

Stephen King suggests taking your first draft and putting it in a drawer (or computer file) for six weeks, so that you have a fresh perspective when you look at it again. I think that's a bit long, but hey, who can argue with Stephen King? The point is that you should let each draft cool off for a bit before you begin your next go-around.

How Long Should It Take to Write the First Draft?

You should write your first draft as *quickly as possible*. I agree with the NaNoWriMo people. Just set yourself a daily page or word goal and hit that goal every day. Do not worry about punctuation or grammar (well, not *too* much) at this stage. Your objective is to get the story on paper.

NaNoWriMo, which I've mentioned before, is an acronym for National Novel Writing Month (nanowrimo.org). It's a terrific idea and a good bunch of people. The concept is simple. Write the first draft of a novel, a minimum of 50,000 words—

a conventional way to determine the length of a novel—in one month. That comes out to 1,661 words a day for a 30-day month. The annual event occurs in the month of November (30 days). I write 2,000 words a day when I'm doing a first draft, so I usually hit my target way in advance of the last day of the month, before Thanksgiving, giving myself something else to be thankful for. I wrote my fifth novel, *The Shadows of Terror* in November of 2014, following the folks at NaNoWriMo. I followed their "rules," and didn't worry about editing as I wrote. After I finished, I read what I wrote. Of course, there were plenty of mistakes because I didn't worry about editing, but I was shocked. *Hey, this is a good story*, I thought. I published the book in March of 2015, four months after I finished my first draft. That sold me on the idea of pushing out the first draft in a hurry. Your job, at that point, is to get the story out, not to come up with a polished manuscript. The NaNoWriMo people send you bits of encouragement along the way, and you can communicate with other writers enrolled in the same month as you. I recommend it if you're working on your first novel. It's like hiring a bunch of cheerleaders, and it doesn't cost anything. That experience sold me. I publish three novels a year, and my first draft usually takes me a month, longer if it's a large book. I don't subscribe to the idea of ignoring editing completely. If you do, when you start on the second draft, you will have a ton of crap to wade through. But don't get hung up with questions like the best word choice, or whether to insert a semicolon or a comma. That's the stuff of rewriting. But doing your first draft in a hurry unfolds the story and starts to show you *THE MAGIC*. It's a great experience.

Rewriting doesn't just mean looking for spelling and grammatical errors. It means finding a better word and eliminating unnecessary words. Cutting down on useless words is critical. Stephen King wrote that he once got a note from an editor which said: "Not bad, but PUFFY. You need to revise for length. Formula: 2nd Draft = 1st Draft − 10%. Good luck." When we're quickly writing draft one, we tend to blather on, inserting lots of unnecessary words. Rewriting also means making sure that your plot and sub-plots make sense. It means that if you're building a town in your book you have sufficient materials to do it. It means polishing your work so that it's the best it can be.

Draft two equals draft one minus ten percent is a rule, but don't take it too literally. The intention is to get you to eliminate unnecessary words. Sometimes (often), on rewrite, you may add a few chapters and a few dozen scenes. There goes the ten percent rule, but don't worry about it. On your next rewrite you will be eliminating the excess words from the new scenes and chapters that you've added. The draft two equals draft one minus 10 percent rule is simply a useful reminder to be concise.

Some Tips to Make Your Editing Better – For you and your editor

I suggest that you use this bag of tricks *after* you've finished your final draft. On each draft you will probably add sections, maybe even chapters, all of which may contain more of the errors you want to avoid. Warning: some of these tips are tedious as hell, but your final product will be all the better. If you ever took one of those online courses that tells you it's easy to write a book—over the weekend—try to get your money back. Writing fiction is a thing of joy, but it takes some real work to bring your joyful book into the light of day. Every day my inbox is stuffed with ads from some scam artist promising that I'll be a millionaire overnight, if I just listen to him—and enroll in his bullshit seminar.

Homophones. Homophones are words that sound alike but are spelled differently and have different meanings. As the words form in your mind, they sometimes find their way to the keyboard in error. We'll now look at common homophones, and what you can do to avoid mixing them.

- **You're, your.** The first is a contraction of "you are," and the second is a possessive pronoun. I suggest that you do a global search on the word "you." This is quite tedious but worth it. The objective is to avoid these mistakes: "*You* voice is perfect;" "You left *you're* money on the dresser." "*Your* going to like this concert." We know the difference between these words, but they have a nasty way of inserting themselves into a manuscript.

- **It's, its.** Many writers will agree that this is one of the most common mistakes we make. As above, the first is a contraction for "it is," and the second is a possessive, as in "Its green color stood out." As I mentioned before, Microsoft Word was plagued with a problem in misplacing these two words. They seem to have gotten their act together.

- **To, too, two.** Substituting "to" for "too" is a common mistake. *To* is a preposition if it expresses motion in a particular direction. "Sally ran *to* the kitchen." *Too* is an adverb that means "to a higher degree than is desirable, permissible, or possible; excessively." "You're driving *too* fast." The secondary meaning of the word is "in addition, also." "I'm coming along *too*." *Two*, of course, is a number.

- **Their, there, they're.** These are popular words to screw up, and that's why we do it so often. *Their* is the possessive case of the pronoun *they*. "I painted their house last week." *There* means "in or at that place." "Put the suitcase *there*." *They're* is a contraction of the words *they are*. "They're coming to take me away." By the way, Microsoft Word just now wanted me to change "their" into "there."

Microsoft Word does not always warn you when you write the wrong word as long as you spell it correctly. In my first novel I wrote a sentence that said, "Seaman Harborrow fired a rifle at the target from a distance of 25 *years*." Whoops, I meant to say 25 *yards*, but it didn't bother Microsoft Word because I spelled years correctly.

Here are a few words that spell-check will pass by as correct, but it can be a disaster for the meaning you intend.

Heroine, heroin; super attendant (superintendent?); loner, loaner; bare, bear. Any others?

Remember, the spell checker on a word processing program is your friend, but *not your best friend.*

The Oxford Comma (aka the Serial Comma or the Harvard Comma)

What is the Oxford Comma? The Oxford comma is the comma that precedes the conjunction before the final item in a list of three or more items.

This song is dedicated to Moe, Larry, and Curly. The comma after Larry is the Oxford Comma. Take out the Oxford comma, and you have a small but confusing mess: This song is dedicated to Moe, Larry and Curly. If you were awarding a prize you would have to present two, not three; one for Moe, and one for Larry and Curly.

"There are people who embrace the Oxford comma and people who don't, and I'll just say this: never get between these people when drink has been taken." Lynne Truss, Eats, Shoots and Leaves (Id. at p. 84).

Yes, it is controversial, and I don't know why. The bottom line: The Oxford comma avoids confusion. For example: "I invited Bill Clinton, George W. Bush and the Hell's Angels." Without the Oxford comma, we are left to wonder what George W. Bush would look like with tattoos and a black leather jacket. Occasionally, the Oxford comma can make a sentence appear awkward. I'll know it when I see it. My default setting is that I always use the Oxford comma. On rewrite, if I come across an awkward sentence that's made awkward by that final comma, I just take it out. Because it's not considered to be a hard and fast rule, it gives me no angst to remove it on rare occasions.

Well Split My Infinitive

An infinitive is the base form of a verb, and comes in two flavors, one beginning with the word "to," and the other without the "to." "To" infinitives include, to sit, to eat, to have, to remember. "Zero" infinitives consist of the preceding words without the "to," as in sit, eat, have, remember. In this section I am limiting myself to "to" infinitives, because that's where the split infinitive problem comes into play. A split infinitive occurs when a word, usually an adverb or an adverbial phrase, comes between the "to" and the base word of the verb. The mother of all split infinitives is the opener for the TV series, *Star Trek*. "*To boldly go* where no man has gone before." In the 19th century, word mavens tried to ban split infinitives entirely. Today, there are still some who insist that infinitives should never be split. But the debate is nowhere as violent as the argument over the Oxford comma. No language guides today insist that you never insert anything between the "to" and the verb root. This whole issue, if there is an issue, is one where the *sound* may be your guide. "To boldly go," or "to go boldly," both sound kind of goofy to me. I'd prefer: "They were bold, and chose to go where no man has gone before." This is your call. Just be aware when you are splitting an infinitive and read it aloud to notice how it sounds.

Sentence Fragments

No problem. A sentence has a subject, object and a predicate. I still recall Sister Mary Whatshername slamming the yardstick across my fingers if I had the temerity to write a sentence without all its parts. The rule against sentence fragments has long ago been abandoned, even in non-fiction. But, and this is a big but, don't write in fragments just for the hell of it, only for a deliberate effect when your style sense demands it. Agreed?

The Politically Correct Personal Pronoun

How do you handle the singular personal pronoun (he or she) when the gender of the person to whom you're referring is unknown? The way to address this conundrum has changed over the years. Let's look at some history.

- **The male pronoun: he, him** - There was a time when the male pronoun was considered universal or generic, having nothing to do with gender, as in *man*kind, the brotherhood of *man*, the dawn of *man*, *man* your battle stations, *man*-up, chair*man*. When a pronoun was called for, you would always use *he* or *him*. You get the picture. You get the picture because these constructions are still quite common. So, in times past, the generic he or him was a simple rule to follow—always use the male personal pronoun unless you're referring to someone who has been identified as a female. If you advocate such usage today you are considered a misogynistic, crypto-fascist, microaggressor, bent on perpetuating male dominance. Well, bullshit. But you can't deny that, as language changes, we feel less comfortable with the male pronoun as a simple automatic set of keystrokes.

- **He or she, him or her – Hedging your bet, Part I.** You see this construction a lot, and it does have the power of logic behind it, if not satisfying style. The person you're referring to may be a man or a woman, and by writing "he or she" you're allowing for the different possibilities. I bet Mr. Spock used this formulation because it's so logical. Problem is, it's awkward as hell, especially if used a lot in a written piece.

- **It Depends on the Gender of the Writer – Males use Male Pronouns, Women use the Female Pronoun**

  Just like the "he or she" construction, this is quite logical, and can be acceptable to the reader, provided the reader knows if you're a guy or a gal. People named Chris or Pat can have a problem.

- **Hedging your bet, Part II – Mix it up.** This has been **my rule** for coping with gender pronouns for years, and you will notice that I use it in the book you're reading. I use the male pronoun in one part of my writing, and switch to the female pronoun on the next page or chapter. I never felt comfortable with the male pronoun used generically and exclusively, and this formulation seems to me an easy way to handle the matter. But stand by for the next section. Maybe take a sip of water first.

- **The Modern Way of Gender Sensitivity, Wherein We Descend into Linguistic Hell.** The authoritative *AP Style Manual* (AP stands for *Associated Press*), the one that's used by journalists rather than the *Chicago Manual of Style*, has dropped a bomb on the English-speaking world. The 2017 Edition magisterially announced that a plural pronoun may be substituted for the male or female pronoun. In an article in *The Weekly Standard*, senior editor Andrew Ferguson showed us the possibilities of linguistic insanity. The article is entitled "The AP's Pronoun Decree – *Everyone* can now do as *they* please." (*The Weekly Standard*, April 17/24, p. 10. emphasis added). He noted that, in a press release, the editors of the APSM said that "they were merely recognizing 'that the spoken language uses they as singular.'" (Id.) Thus, because a lot of people speak incorrect English, an authoritative style guide changed the rules—for no logical reason other than to follow the pack. So, we now see inflicted upon the English language sentences like these: "The *student* needs to improve *their* grade if they want to graduate." Or, "The *student* hurt *themself.*" Or "The *student* hurt *theirself.*" You can't make this shit up—nor would you want to. If this trajectory holds true, in a hundred years or so we'll be back to communicating by grunts and hand gestures.

Do not End a Sentence with a Preposition – We learned this in elementary school. Well, some of us did, and it's one of the rules in *The Elements of Style*. Winston Churchill (although there is some dispute whether he actually wrote this) is purported to have said about the prohibition of ending a sentence with a preposition, "This is the type of arrant pedantry *up with which I will not put.*" This sounds like the kind of witticism that Churchill would write. Whoever actually said it, the quote puts the issue to bed. Here's a rule you should follow: Avoid ending a sentence with a preposition, *unless it makes sense to do so.*

Chapter 12

A Time-Saver You Should Consider

Macros – A short-cut to words that you use a lot. Leap Frog Your Keyboard

I strongly recommend a wonderful little piece of software called "Shortkeys," sold by Insight Software Solutions (www.shortkeys.com). They give you a 30-day free trial, after which you can buy it for $29.95. It's a "macro generator," which means that it turns long words or even sentences and keyboard procedures into a simple set of two or three keystrokes. Setup is easy. You create a Shortkey phrase that's easy to type and remember. In one of my books, a character named MacPherson appeared often, along with other members of his family. MacPherson is 10 letters long and is a tricky word to type. With Shortkeys, I named him "ma." To call up the Shortkey you simply place a "z" in front of the phrase to make it a Shortkey. So, I type in "zma" and out comes "MacPherson." The disable function is easy to use and important. In the book where the MacPherson family constantly appeared I also had a chapter where the word "hazmat," short for "hazardous materials," appeared often. Each time I began to type hazmat, Shortkeys saw the "zma" and thought I wanted MacPherson. So, appeared "hazMacPherson." I just disabled the "ma" shortkey temporarily with two keystrokes, and enabled it when I was done with the hazardous materials chapter. Another great time saver with Shortkeys is that it isn't just for word processing programs but works on the Internet wherever you need to input words. This is a fantastic way of saving time when filling out a form online, something we writers do all the time. You can make a Shortkey for your address, your name, your email address, phone number, each of your books, and so on. When filling out forms that require you to input your book title, the program is a Godsend. One of my books, a bit of a mouthful, has a shortkey of zjia, which equals *Justice in America: How it Works - How it Fails.*

How about "zcop?" On my computer it now means "Copyright © 2018 by Russell F. Moran – All Rights Reserved." I just need to remember to change the date once a year. If you're filling out a form for one of the countless book sites on the Internet, Shortkeys will save you an enormous amount of time. You not only make a Shortkey for your address and phone number, but also for the book you're promoting. On my computer "zgra" means *The Gray Ship.* I had to disable the Shortkey "zgra" to illustrate this for you. Here are a few of my Shortkey time savers:

My email address is "zem"

My name and address is "zadd"

My first name is "zru" (Russell)

My last name is "zmo" (Moran)

My phone number is "zph"

My website is "zww" (http://www.morancom.com)

My corporation is"zmci" (Moran Communications, Inc.)

The book you are reading is "znov," *The Novel—A Writer's Guide—Discover the Joy of Writing Fiction.*

I think you see the picture. As a writer in this time of frenetic activity, something that saves time is a gift. Get this program (www.shortkeys.com). It's a great investment for 30 bucks.

A hint. Sometimes (rarely) Shortkeys stops working. Simple solution. Close the program and re-open it.

Chapter 13

About Chapters and Paragraphs

Chapter - A chapter is a section of a book that addresses one theme, although this is not a hard and fast rule.

When changing a theme, however, you don't always want to begin a new chapter. Just create a *sub-chapter or a section*. Do this with three asterisks centered on the page, like this:

***

You should have a paragraph break before and after the asterisks. PLEASE Note. For some annoying reason, Microsoft Word will string a bunch of dots across the page when you hit the enter key after the three asterisks. No problem. Just hit the backspace key and the dots go away. Hit backspace once again and your cursor is where you want it to be.

Paragraph - Think of a paragraph as a stream of thoughts or ideas that are related. If you change the thought, it's time for a new paragraph.

DANGER – Avoid the never-ending paragraph. The Internet and email have changed the way we read, and now we expect shorter paragraphs. Think back a few years ago, if you're old enough, to a time when you read the morning mail, and that was about it for communications directed to you for that day, not counting TV ads.

Now we're inundated with non-stop messages, some needing action, others that require reading because the subject is important. Imagine that you just received an email from somebody with whom you serve on a committee. The message is one long ocean of words with no paragraph breaks, although the thoughts and themes covered in the message change constantly. That message should carry the words in the subject line: "Do not read this message," or "Read this message later, if you can find the time," or when reading a novel, "skip this paragraph."

I use the email example because I think you can easily relate to what I just said. Now, think of an advertising email you received from a talented copywriter. The paragraphs are short even though the message can go on for 10 typewritten pages. You keep reading because each paragraph makes you interested in reading the next one. That's one of the reasons why copywriters are paid a lot of money, and we buy a lot of useless crap.

The exact same analysis holds for a novel. A page covered with words and no paragraph breaks slows you down as you're reading, even making your eyes feel the need for sleep. What if you need to pee in the middle of one of these endless word attacks? It places a burden on a reader, the last thing you ever want to do.

Some writing pundits have come up with rules—God knows where they get some of these rules. One "rule" says that a *paragraph can never consist of only one sentence*, or, oh my goodness, a *single word*.

Bullshit.

A paragraph should consist of as many or as few sentences or words as your writer's eye demands, or the stream of thought requires. The important thing to keep in mind is the reader's experience. Make your words, sentences, and paragraphs easy to read.

How to Keep the Pages Turning — Set up the Next Chapter

How many times have you read something like the following at the end of a chapter in a good book?

"Rick's leg was throbbing in pain. He didn't know that in a few minutes something would happen make him forget about his leg."

"The dinner party was everything Harry and Meg expected, and they went to bed feeling happy and proud. The next morning's newspaper headline made them forget their wonderful evening."

"Matt didn't know what was in the package. He was too tired to open it that night. When he opened it the next morning, his life would change forever."

"As they stood on the dock sipping cocktails, they were unaware of the giant fish swimming at them."

"Alice threw her arms around Sam's neck and kissed him, not knowing that it was the last time she would ever see him."

The idea should be obvious. A cliffhanging sentence at the end of a chapter makes for the "page-turning experience" that you see in positive reviews. This same thought holds true for the length of a chapter, as the late Tom Clancy knew so well. Clancy's chapters tended to be short, with endings pulling you to read the next chapter. That's why his books are so exciting—and sell so many copies, many years after his death.

What is the Best Length for a Paragraph?

The simple answer to the question posed is that the paragraph should be the length it *needs to be*, not some rule imposed by an expert.

A paragraph should consist of as many or as few sentences or words as your writer's eye demands. The important thing to keep in mind is the reader's experience.

Chapter 14

Tips, Tricks—Things to do—Things to Avoid

In this chapter I review tips and warnings that you should be aware of as you write your novel, and definitely as you go through the process of rewriting and editing.

Some of my All Time Favorite Typos

I call these typos favorites because I commit them so often I must like them. Here are a few of the little bastards:

- The the
- is is
- a a
- ., (period comma)
- ,. (comma period)
- .. (double period. This is a common typing mistake. I committed this error two paragraphs above as my editor pointed out.

The best way to find these is after you've finished your final draft (Yes, there is such a thing as a final draft). Do a global search on each of them, such as, the(space)the, is(space)is, a(space)a, .(period period). You will be amazed at how often these suckers pop up. This is nowhere near as tedious as the global search for the word 'you,' and it's a procedure you should employ after the "final draft."

Adverbs

Any writing expert will tell you that excessive use of adverbs shows a lazy and sloppy way of writing. What this means is that you should use great caution when adding an adverb to a sentence. It does not mean that you should eliminate adverbs entirely. (Note the adverb "entirely). I could have written, "in all cases," but I left the adverb to illustrate my point). You should question each use of an adverb used in fiction and see if it's needed. Nine times out of ten it can be tossed, but it's often just fine in dialog—because that's how people speak. So, here's the tip, and yes, it's tedious. Do a global search on "ly," and ask yourself if the word is needed each time. Not all adverbs end in "ly," but those that do announce themselves. A few adverbs that don't end in "ly" include, never, often, and very (more on the word *very* in the next section, below). Really. When you come upon an adverb as you edit, I suggest that you cut the word out so that your eyes can see what the sentence looks like without the adverb. You'll be amazed that *90 percent of the time*, the sentence works better without the adverb. You can always paste the word back in if you think it's needed.

I read the following sentence in a book: "Bill opened the door strongly, walked across the floor angrily, and sat down suddenly." If there is a place called "adverb hell," that sentence resides there. The sentence also violated the principle of "show don't tell." The author of that slop *told* us what Bill experienced, and in no way did he *show* it to us. How about this sentence instead? "Bill opened the door, slamming it against the wall. He walked across the floor, threw his hat on the table, and sat down with a thud, knocking a coffee mug off the table as he did."

Some pundits will tell you to eliminate *all* adverbs. That's stupid advice— *really* stupid. Sometimes an adverb just does the trick. Sometimes, but more often not. Stephen King wrote that "The road to hell is paved with adverbs and I will shout it from the rooftops." (King, Stephen. *On Writing: A Memoir of The Craft* (Kindle Location 1519). Scribner. Kindle Edition.) But even Master Stephen admits that sometimes an adverb is necessary, or at least desirable.

The Word *Very* – The Adverb from Hell (or is it?)

Conventional wisdom among many writers holds that the word "very" is poisonous, a useless word that clouds your writing, adding an unnecessary emphasis when you could achieve the same thing with a more powerful word. Substitute "outraged" for "very angry."

I believe that hatred of the word *very* began with Mark Twain, a man who loathed the word. I refer to very haters as *very Nazis*, because they attack with a mindless and totalitarian vigor. Just google "should I use the word very" and you'll see the venom spewed by people who should consider getting a life.

Twain famously said, "Substitute 'damn' every time you're inclined to write 'very;' your editor will delete it and the writing will be just as it should be." In his day, the word "damn" was considered vulgar.

But, like many "rules" of writing, this one has become overdone. The author and columnist Charles Murray, for example, in his *Curmudgeon's Guide to Getting Ahead*, advocates performing a global search and delete every appearance of the word. "As for *very*," Murray writes, "you may, if you insist, take a look at each occurrence before deleting. But hardly any of them should survive."

Well, I feel duly chastised for believing that a word in the English language has a reason to exist. Very is both an adjective and an adverb, and sometimes, not often but sometimes, it's just the right word.

As an adjective, we see it used (to the horror of the purists) in a sentence such as, "I visited the *very* school that I attended when I lived in England."

As an adverb, and this is where the purists come down with the vapors, we see it in a sentence such as, "He was *very* tall." A *very Nazi* would substitute, "He was tall as a skyscraper," or some other such literary *bon mot*.

The late writer (and grouch) Florence King once said: "'Very' is the most useless word in the English language and can always come out. More than useless, it is treacherous because it invariably weakens what it is intended to strengthen." That this sentence made no sense was lost on Florence King.

Very Nazis don't feel the need to convince you of their logic. They are satisfied to denounce any use of the word very with puritanical vigor. So there.

In one of my novels, I wrote a scene where a new CIA agent tries to convince her superior that she should be allowed to use hand grenades in an upcoming raid on terrorists. After showing him that she understood the weapon, she then hit him with the clincher: "And I have a *very* strong throwing arm." As an exercise, I tried my best to come up with a way for her to convince her boss without the use of the word very. I couldn't. She was simply emphasizing that her strong throwing arm was quite strong. Well, it as *very* strong. Take out the word, and the sentence would suffer, with all due apologies to Mark Twain, Florence King, and the goose-stepping hordes of very Nazis. A dedicated purist would have me substitute a strong word in place of very, such as, "She had an arm like a rocket." Well pardon me, but she didn't have an arm like a friggin rocket, and it would be awkward for her to say this to her boss. No, she had a strong throwing arm. How strong? *Very* strong. Think of the word as an *intensifier*. In my example above, the word very intensified the strong throwing arm.

So here is the rule that I follow concerning the word very: Use the word sparingly, *very* sparingly if you will. You may want to restrict it to dialogue. The reason it belongs in dialogue is because that's the way real people speak. A bad report card will result in a parent telling a kid that she is "very disappointed," not "quite disappointed," not "hugely disappointed," but *very* disappointed. Moms say stuff like that.

The best rule of writing is this: Don't become a slave to a rule. *Sieg Heil*, baby.

Some More about Qualifiers and Intensifiers

Just as I said about the intensifier "very" above, you should only use intensifiers or qualifiers if necessary, and usually they aren't.

Trust yourself to make a statement without adding qualifiers such as "pretty," "somewhat," or "arguably." Besides "very," watch out for other common intensifiers, such as "extremely," or "absolutely." You're trying to force your thoughts on the reader. Don't worry. Your readers will get what you're saying if you say it well.

Example: "Tom Brady is an extremely talented quarterback, and his passing statistics absolutely place him at the top of the league."

Better: "Tom Brady is the best quarterback in the NFL."

Also, use the **exclamation point** sparingly if at all. I once read an opinion that an exclamation point is like a writer laughing at his own joke.

Don't Repeat Words in Close Proximity.

Unless you repeat the same word for style reasons, avoid repeating words in close proximity. The following sentence is okay, because it's done for style: "I never drink lemonade, never buy it, and never allow it into my house." That sentence is written to express the author's distaste for lemonade, and the repetition of the word *"never"* is justified on style grounds. But how about this sentence? "I tried that once, but it didn't work, so I decided that I would try that again." Ugh. How about: "I tried but it didn't work, so I did it over."

Sage advice often given is that you should read your words aloud when you're editing or rewriting. When I was a law review editor, the standard practice for reviewing an article was for two student editors take turns reading aloud to one another. That's probably why law students drink so much. But, tedious as it may be, the process works. If you read out loud, repeated words stand out as poor writing. Proximity of repeated words doesn't just mean within the same sentence. You should avoid too many repetitions in adjacent sentences, or even in the same paragraph. For example, "I took the boat down the river looking for a boat ramp. Not finding one, I tied the boat to a pole alongside a pier. When I climbed onto the pier, I made sure to cover the boat with canvas." Let's try to make this repetitious scene work. "I ~~took the boat~~ **motored** down the river looking for a ~~boat~~ ramp. Not finding one, I tied ~~the boat~~ **up** to a pole alongside a pier. When I climbed onto the pier, I made sure to cover the boat with canvas." Even though I deleted three references to the word "boat," the reader, if he's from planet earth, is still clear that I'm talking about a boat.

Use simple words. Don't use a seventy-five cent word when a nickel word will do.

Please don't try to convince the reader that you're brilliant. This suggestion is similar to the admonition to "Murder your darlings." Use a simple word when it will do the job.

- Live, not reside

- Buy, not purchase

- Have, not possess

- Use, not utilize

- Person, not individual

I also suggest avoiding the use of "one" as an indication of a second person. "One loves the springtime because it signals renewal." People who talk like that drink tea with a raised pinky finger. Better to say: "We love the springtime because it signals renewal."

Chapter 15

Dialog – *You Talkin to Me?*

Crafting dialog is one of the true joys of writing fiction. Note that I used the word "craft." I did so because I want to convey that dialog is much more than characters on a page talking to each other. You use dialog to tell the story, to create scenes, to develop characters who aren't just words on a page. They are people, real people, if you will only let them be. As an aside, I want to share a Tweet with you, one that I found motivating, even moving. "Goodnight friends," the Twitter user said, "I have to get back to writing my novel and save a few lives. Without me my characters will die." Did I mention that writing fiction is magical?

For the past few years we have heard that we live in the Golden Age of Television. I mentioned this before when I discussed the competition for our time. I try to keep my TV time to a minimum, but I must agree with the phrase. The reason TV is in a Golden Age is because of the writers. Good actors and directors have been around for a long time, but the story lines of some of the top TV shows are gems. *Blue Bloods* on CBS is one of my favorites. As in a well-written novel, the writers give us scenes and characters that seem to be a part of our lives. My favorite segment of every show is the "dining room scene," where Police Commissioner Frank Reagan (Tom Seleck) sits down with his large family and discusses the day's events. Two of his sons are cops, his father is a former police commissioner, and his daughter is an assistant DA, so they often talk shop. They laugh, yell, pass compliments, and occasionally insult each other. The writers pull this off so well and with such realism that you almost want to say, "Please pass the potatoes." The impact on the viewer is the same as the impact on a reader of a well-written novel. Dialog is one of the critical keys to a good novel, and there are some definite rules. I hope I won't bore you by saying this, but don't worry about rules. That said, I don't advocate that you break rules just for the sake of breaking them. Let your creativity be in control. As I discussed before about the hated word *very*, be careful when you break a rule and stop and think if it's necessary. If so, break the rule. So, let's look at some rules of dialog.

- **Each speaker gets a new paragraph**, no matter how short. I can see no reason why anybody would want to break this rule, so just follow it. Each speaker gets a paragraph. Don't deprive them. Also, it makes it much clearer for the reader who is talking.

- **Dialog attribution.** *He said, she said, I said.* "Said" is the preferable word here, but sometimes it's a good idea to break the rule. The reason it's a good rule is that it tells you who's speaking, and the word "said" is almost invisible to the reader. Identify the speaker only if necessary. If just two people are talking, it's often obvious who's the speaker.

So, in a scene where John and Nancy talk, you write, "You look well-rested this morning, John." It's not necessary and a complete waste of words to write "she said." or "Nancy said." If there are more than two people in the scene, make sure you identify the speaker if it's not obvious from the preceding sentence. As a general rule—*general*—try to stick with the word "said," or occasionally, "asked." Don't try to be fancy for no reason. Write "I'm going to the store," John said, not *John informed us* or *John pointed out.*

Your own style, as always, should be your final guide. "I'm going to the store," John said—you may add —"as he jumped onto his motorcycle"—thereby giving the scene a bit of a visual lift. Take the great novelist Nelson DeMille, for example: "Go fuck yourself," John Corey *recommended.*" Much better than "said," and a lot funnier.

Make sure you don't put quotation marks around John said, he said, or she said. And put a comma after the sentence that the character said, NEVER a period. "I'm going for a swim, (comma)" Jane said.

- **Avoid talking heads**. Sometimes a scene or the story itself requires two people to talk to each other at some length. You need to break up the words with some visual showing. "We should go, Nancy. It's time for the wake."

The paragraph belongs to Nancy (remember, each speaker gets a paragraph), and she can use it without saying words. *Nancy said nothing. She stared at the floor. When she looked up I could see a tear running down her face.* Also, notice how this is showing not telling. We know that Nancy's sad and upset without the author telling us. Sometimes a character says a lot by saying nothing. Talking heads belong at the counter in a diner, not in your book. If the scene does require two people to say a lot back and forth to each other, split is up by showing the reader what's going on. Instead of just John said, how about *John said as he poured himself another beer.* Or *Mary said, as she threw an empty beer can at John.* Something like this breaks the monotony of two heads talking. Also, it *shows* the scene.

- **Characters should talk the way real people talk.** "We must evaluate this new set of circumstances," John said. Better: "We gotta check this out," John said. Again, this is why it's a good idea to read your manuscript out loud, to yourself or to somebody else. The phrase "stilted language" in a review means that the characters don't seem real, at least not based on the way they talk.

- **Using Profanity** - Sometimes vulgarity is called for. If you find yourself turned off by cuss words, you must live in a different world. So, a guy walks into a room carrying a large bowl of hot pasta sauce. He trips and the sauce goes flying across the floor, creating a huge mess and screwing up dinner plans. "Gee whizz. I dropped the darn thing," he said. I don't think so. A character in one of my books is a beautiful, caring woman who has a PhD in engineering and is a professor at a university. Her only fault is that she talks, as her husband observes, "like a cab driver in traffic." By having this smart, good-looking woman dropping f-bombs all over the place, I created a character who's not easy to forget. Good fiction involves a lot of tension, in plot, in characters, and in the whole story itself. I created tension with this character by having her speak in a way you wouldn't expect. No shit.

Chapter 16

How to End Your Novel

Just as the beginning of a novel is important, the end is also one of the items that requires your utmost attention and imagination.

A novel doesn't need to have a happy ending, but it should *satisfy* the reader. The most important consideration for the end of your book should be an element of surprise, or an emotional jolt. A happy ending is just fine, but it must seem real, otherwise the Internet trolls will give you bad reviews.

Unexpected. That's the keyword for a good ending. If, on page 250 of a 325 page book, your reader can figure out the ending, you haven't done your job.

In Gillian Flynn's novel, *Gone Girl,* you will find just such an unexpected ending. I won't be a spoiler in case you ever read this fine book, but you will be shocked when, at the end of the story, you realize you are being spoken to by a psychopath.

Here are just a few sample endings for bringing a satisfying jolt to your reader:

- Your hero wakes up and it was all a bad dream. CAUTION. This is a common story thread—recall

The Wizard of Oz. But, if handled properly, it can still work.

- Your hero successfully slays the dragons and the village people carry him on their shoulders, cheering. Endings don't get much cornier than this. Consider celebrating the hero in a more subtle way. Remember Kevin Costner playing Elliott Ness in *The Untouchables?* He overcomes Al Capone and the evil mobsters, and saves America from the devil booze. At the end of the movie, the writers could have placed him in an auditorium full of government agents cheering him after he gives a rousing speech. Instead, at the end, Elliott Ness is asked, having found out that the 18th Amendment (the Prohibition Law) has been repealed, what he intends to do now. "I think I'll have a drink," Ness said.

- Your hero gets a letter from a villain he thought was dead.

- Your hero's brilliant idea for slaying the dragon gets reversed on the last page, by some unforeseen event.

- Your hero, lying in a hospital bed thinking all is lost, gets a surprise visit from (a long-lost son or daughter, an old boyfriend, an old girlfriend, or maybe her aunt who she thought was dead), and finds out that her elaborate plan worked after all, even though she has a fractured whatever.

- Your hero gets killed. Use extreme caution here. Readers love heroes and killing somebody your reader loves can be a problem. With an ending like this you may consider two heroes (husband-and-wife detectives, fellow soldiers, passengers on an ill-fated cruise ship?). One of the heroes solves the problem (maybe kills the bad guys that caused hero number one's death). If you just kill off a hero and leave a bunch of sub-plots dangling, that makes for an unsatisfactory ending. Tragedy is okay, a theme that's honored in Western literature; just make it satisfying. If you leave your reader feeling bummed out at the end of your book, don't expect her to buy your next one.

If you plan to write a series, the end of your book should sell your next book. Like a cliff hanger at the end of a chapter to nudge the reader to the next one, this is a way to encourage your reader to buy your next book. Amazon makes it so easy, and if the book in question is an ebook, your reader may buy it and start to read your next one within minutes of finishing the first. I do that often. Please note that I'm not advocating that you write a series that can only be read *as a series*, not as stand-alone books. That's playing games with your readers, games that you will never win. I mentioned E.M. Foner's series of sci-fi comedies earlier. Each of the 14 novels in his *EarthCent Ambassador* series can be read as a stand-alone book. Same goes for my five-book series, *The Time Magnet*.

Writing fiction is magic. It's a joy, if you allow it to be. I often tell people that reality is overrated. With fiction, I get to improve on the world, scene by scene.

So when will you begin your journey? After dinner, after a walk, maybe later, maybe tomorrow, maybe after you reread this book?

How about now? Yes, that's *RIGHT NOW*. You can't edit or rewrite something that hasn't been written.

Here's to your magical experience.

A Note from the Author

As you can probably tell from reading *The Novel - A Writer's Guide - Discover the Joy of Writing Fiction,* that I love to write, and I hope that this book will help your writing career and bring as much joy to you as it has to me. I have a request, if you don't mind. **Please consider leaving a review on Amazon.com** or your favorite book site. As you embark on your writing life, you will find that reviews are the lifeblood of a book, whether it's a novel or a work of nonfiction.

My Novels

All books are available on Amazon.com, and also as ebooks on The Kindle or a Kindle app for your phone or iPad.

The Gray Ship –
Book One of *The Time Magnet Series*

http://amzn.to/16GPumH

"This provocative, intensely powerful novel is a must-read for sci-fi fans and Civil War aficionados, though mainstream fiction readers will find it heart-rending and inspiring as well. A rare read that's not only wildly entertaining, but also profoundly moving." — Kirkus Reviews

The Thanksgiving Gang –
Book Two of *The Time Magnet Series*

"I had never read a book before written http://amzn.to/1NzBs7N in an efficient, minimalistic prose... Instead of writing what most readers want to read, he gives voice to life-like characters, with their flaws and prejudices. They are not infallible superheroes. It's always nice to find a new voice in fiction and to enjoy creativity at its best." — C. Ludewig. "Breakneck pacing and virtually nonstop action" – Kirkus Reviews

A Time of Fear – \
Book Three of *The Time Magnet Series*

http://amzn.to/1zdjaG9

"His story is fascinating and adds even more depth to this already cavernously deep novel. Amazingly unique, chilling and well written, Moran weaves a future that is both desperate and hopeful. Blending modern fears with science fiction results in a tale that will keep you reading long into the night." Five stars!"
—Heather

The Skies of Time –
Book Four of *The Time Magnet Series*

http://amzn.to/1CCC3jg

In *The Skies of Time*, you will recognize the two main characters, Ashley Patterson, now an admiral, and her husband, Jack Thurber. They met and fell in love in *The Gray Ship*, and now they're in for the adventure of their lives in *The Skies of Time*. Ashley and Jack have been such prominent characters in all five books of The Time Magnet Series that I feel like they're old friends. You will also recognize some of the other characters. But if I told you who they are, it would ruin the fun.

"I'm big fan of this series and this one may be the best. I hope there is another book to this series since it keeps getting better. There are a few questions I have about certain events that makes the next one even more suspenseful. These are great books to binge read one after the other."   Time Travel Fan

The Shadows of Terror –
Book One of the *Patterns Series*

http://amzn.to/1IDQzJS

A novel that explodes off the front page of your newspaper.

Terrorism now has a new face, a face that's obscured in the shadows. The radical forces of destruction have learned to make themselves invisible to the West, and preventing a terrorist attack has become almost impossible.

A new war has begun, World War III.

Rick Bellamy, an FBI agent who specializes in counterterrorism, is engaged in his own war, a war with no end.

Bellamy's wife, Ellen, a prominent architect, discovers that she's in the middle of the greatest terror plot to date.

To defeat the enemy, Bellamy first needs to uncover the clues, to shine a light on the shadows. He has to find patterns – before it's too late.

"Move over James Patterson and Mary Higgins Clark. There's a new guy in town. Russ Moran's new book – *The Shadows of Terror.*" — Frank from Lynbrook

The Scent of Revenge -
Book Two in the *Patterns Series.*

http://amzn.to/1UvDRmw

The world is at war with the forces of terror. FBI Agent Rick Bellamy and his wife, Ellen, find themselves in the middle of a sinister terrorist plot.

Someone is attacking young prominent women, inflicting a horrible disease that mimics Alzheimer's.

Nobody knows its origin, nobody knows how to stop it, nobody knows how to cure it.

Rick Bellamy and a team of FBI agents and scientists want to go on offense. But how?

Will the lives of the women be changed forever? When will the attacks stop?

"Heart pounding, can't put down thriller that will force you to look at terrorism in different light. Life in America will never be the same." —Cold Coffee Café

Sideswiped -
Book One in the Matt Blake series of legal thrillers.

http://amzn.to/1MkxX35

Trial lawyer Matt Blake took on a perfect case.

It involved a sideswipe collision in which his client's husband, an investigative reporter, was killed. The evidence of negligence was overwhelming. Eyewitnesses testified that defendant was talking on his cellphone when he hit the other car.

But was it negligence? Was it an accident?

Or was it murder?

Matt uncovers evidence that the act may have been intentional. Somebody wanted the man silenced. Somebody wanted the man dead. Somebody had a lot to hide.

The signs started to point to the highest levels of government.

An open-and-shut personal injury case suddenly became a vast conspiracy of terror.

"This book hooks you in from the first line. *Sideswiped* draws you into the world of Matt Blake and you become emotionally attached to him and his journey. The story itself is so well-written and so fast-moving there is never a dull moment." — Sarah Elle

"Moran demonstrates the depth of his writing talent by developing a new genre with *Sideswiped*, a legal thriller. Branching out from his previous novels dealing with time travel, Moran goes in a whole new direction with Book One in the Matt Blake series. He creates a wild but totally believable story of modern day intrigue and suspense. Moran also deftly weaves into this book some of my favorite characters from his prior novels. I am looking forward to starting Book #2 - *The Reformers* — A Kindle customer

The Reformers -

Book Two of the Matt Blake series of legal thrillers, is the sequel to *Sideswiped*.

http://amzn.to/2m8uMdu

The forces of radical Islam are on the run.

Their leadership has been decimated, their ranks thinned, their power disappearing by the week.

Their recruiting efforts have been cut off, the radical websites shut down, and the attraction of jihad is losing its appeal among the young.

With targeted assassinations, military strikes, as well as the loss of oil fields and gold mines, radical Islam is fast losing power.

But who is responsible?

It isn't the United States Government. It's a new force the world has never seen before.

Lawyer Matt Blake and his wife Diana find themselves in the middle of the most gigantic plot the world has ever seen, a conspiracy that's only begun to grow.

"I've been a fan of the author, Russell Moran, since reading *Sideswiped* a few months ago, so I admittedly went into this book with quite high expectations. That being said, I had no idea that *"The Reformers"* was going to play out in the way that it did and I can see myself giving this book a re-read in the future. In fact, I am even more impressed by the storyline of this read than the last and it has left me excited to see more." Lucidity.

The Keepers of Time –

Book Five of the Time Magnet Series

http://amzn.to/2wjVSTt

Admiral Ashley Patterson and her husband Jack have done it again. They've traveled through time, 200 years into the future—aboard a nuclear aircraft carrier, Ashley's flagship.

They discover a new world, a strange new world—a post-nuclear war world—one that is both a beacon of hope, and a cry of despair.

They meet a group of people who call themselves *The Keepers of Time,* an organization dedicated to preserving history and culture.

But the world around them has harkened back to a primitive and savage past, one that includes human sacrifice.

Ashley knows they have to have to get back to the present to warn the government of the unspeakable horrors that await.

But finding the way back to the present is their greatest challenge, an almost insurmountable one.

"A wild time travel yarn that starts fast and doesn't slow down until the end."

A Reunion in Time

http://amzn.to/2tneIsg

What if a 37-year-old adult travels back 20 years in time and finds himself in high school, followed by his 36-year-old wife? They're now teenagers, 17 and 16.

Adults in teenage bodies, they struggle to convince the people from their past that they are real, not apparitions. With the benefit of hindsight, they know the history of the past 20 years, and it isn't pretty.

Rick and Ellen are married, and now have to adjust to married life as teenagers in 2001. Rick is a senior FBI official and Ellen is a famous architect.

But everybody sees them as kids. Nobody believes that they're married, and nobody believes their stories—until Rick and Ellen predict 9/11.

How do they find their way back to the year they came from? How do they warn the authorities of another cataclysm that will occur in the future? The answer is to find the time portal—the wormhole—that brought them to 2001. But the site has changed. It's no longer the place where they crossed the wormhole. Will they live out the balance of their lives beginning as teenagers? "We've all wish we could go back to earlier times with the mind we have now. This Russell Moran book takes you there and it is a fun creative romp well worth reading. *A Reunion in Time* is highly recommended!" Kindle Customer.

The President is Missing

Book Three of the Matt Blake series. Published in May, 2017.

http://amzn.to/2t9v7wu

While he was addressing the nation from a submerged nuclear submarine, President Blake's message is suddenly cut off. Anyone listening heard an explosion. The explosion was followed by floating debris five minutes later.

First Lady Dee Blake has doubts, which she shares with naval high command and the new president. She thinks the explosion and the debris were a ruse to make people think the sub was destroyed, and her husband with it.

Could the sub have been hijacked and the president kidnapped?

But who would commit such an act? What is its purpose?

Was it Russia, China, Iran, or a shadowy group of freelance terrorists?

The new president appoints Dee as his Chief of Staff, with explicit instructions to find the missing submarine—and President Matt Blake.

Her life, and the life of the nation, suddenly take a horrifying turn.

"This was a wonderfully dramatic story by Moran, and it keeps the reader on the edge of the seat. A real page turner. Filled with conspiracies, nuclear weapons and the President, this story takes a turn as the First Lady embarks on a journey to find the truth. It's one of those stories that you want to savor every word and are being pulled in. The characters are strong and well-developed. A magnificently explosive story. A must-have for any bookshelf." Amy Shannon

Robot Depot
http://amzn.to/2zXW7C2

Mike Bateman is a visionary businessman, the creator and CEO of the fabulously successful chain of stores, Robot Depot, a company dedicated to selling robots and Artificial Intelligence machines for a variety of uses.

The company is a darling of Wall Street and is the most popular destination for consumers and businesses looking for labor saving devices.

But the company caught the eye of ISIS, the terrorist Islamic State. They discover a great way to deliver bombs – using the products of Robot Depot to kill people.

Robot Depot changed from being a popular company to an object of fear because of the tampered products it sells. The terrorists use the company for "terror spectaculars," including the destruction of a skyscraper, a drone attack on Yankee Stadium, and the bombing of a children's sailing regatta.

Mike Bateman and the FBI are in a race to stop his products from becoming weapons, a race to stop the wanton killings. His wife and partner, Jenny, discovers the true meaning of terror one horrible summer day.

"Robot Depot is a twisting romp on a great premise. I truly enjoyed this book. Many Characters that I have come to enjoy." Rick S.

A Climate of Doubt

https://amzn.to/2KCvv3e

A book that looks at the horrors of climate change, and how it became a weapon of terrorism. Matt and Dee Blake take on their biggest challenge to date, along with our old friends, Rick and Ellen Bellamy. A book about the evils of science, terrorism, and international intrigue.

"A Compelling Read. Moran does a masterful job of crafting an action-packed, suspenseful read about the devastating consequences of climate manipulation. The diabolical mastermind behind the caper is a dictator of the worst kind—a man without conscience who cares only for power. Through the magic of Moran's digital pen, the men and woman in white hats are three-dimensional and vividly real. While this is a work of fiction, it's plausible fiction. We can easily relate to the horrific consequences of such an act of terrorism as so capably portrayed in Mr. Moran's prose." Colorado Avid Reader

The Maltese Incident
Book One of the Harry and Meg Series

https://amzn.to/2lZTvyA

A corporate cruise ship, *The Maltese*, sets sail from Manhattan for the beautiful Azores on a charity fundraising cruise. The ship encounters a strange event in the ocean, and, after two minutes of turbulence, finds itself in a different time. The ship is surrounded by gigantic sharks. They've traveled back in time millions of years.

The captain, Harry Fenton, a highly decorated naval war hero, falls in love with a beautiful passenger. After a whirlwind romance, they marry—in the ship's ballroom. Captain Fenton convinces the passengers and crew that they must move ashore to a tropical island because the ship is running out of fuel and supplies.

An ancient forest inhabited by dinosaurs awaits them.

Will the 1,000 souls ever make it back to the time they came from, or will they remain stranded in the distant past?

Realizing that their lives have hit the reset button, the crew and passengers construct a community in the forest—Malta Town. They begin their new lives—among the dinosaurs.

The Maltese Incident is a tale of time travel, love, courage, and horror.

A Request

If you enjoyed *The Novel - A Writer's Guide - Discover the Joy of Writing Fiction*, please consider leaving a brief review on amazon.com. Reviews are an author's lifeblood.

About the Author

Russ Moran is the author of 15 novels.

- *The Gray Ship,* Book One of *The Time Magnet* series, is a story of time travel, alternate history, romance, and a nuclear warship that finds itself in the Civil War. *The Thanksgiving Gang* is the sequel, *A Time of Fear* is Book Three, *The Skies of Time* is Book Four, and *The Keepers of Time* is book five.

- *The Shadows of Terror* is Book One of The Patterns series, followed by *The Scent of Revenge.*

- *A Reunion in Time* is a time travel novel, but not in the Time Magnet series.

- *Sideswiped,* a legal thriller, is Book One of the Matt Blake Series.

- *The Reformers* is Book Two of the Matt Blake Series, and *The President is Missing* is Book Three.

- *Robot Depot,* is a novel about our automated future, was published in September 2017.

I also published six nonfiction books: *Justice in America: How it Works—How it Fails; The APT Principle: The Business Plan That You Carry in Your Head; Boating Basics: The Boattalk Book of Boating Tips; If You're Injured: A Consumer Guide to Personal Injury Law; How to Create More Time; The Novel - A Writer's Guide - Discover the Joy of Writing Fiction*

Russ is a lawyer and a veteran of the United States Navy. He lives on Long Island, New York, with his wife and editor, Lynda.

www.ingramcontent.com/pod-product-compliance
Lightning Source LLC
Chambersburg PA
CBHW071002040426
42443CB00007B/624